GOD'S
GAME
PLAN

Tom Stahler

Rev 14:14-16

ISBN: 0-9649219-3-6 softcover

Library of Congress Catalog Number: 97-090986

Published by:
Times Ten Publishing
PO Box 36
White Pine, Michigan 49971

Printed by
Eerdmans Printing Company
231 Jefferson SE
Grand Rapids, Michigan 49503

WELCOME

TO

GOD'S
GAME
PLAN

Other books by Tom Steinbach:

Now That Forever Has Ended*

*a powerful historical novel

TO YOU

In dedication to
all who read this book
with the desire to
learn and profit
from it...thus
to you, my
friend
☐

Also to Florence Steinbach, my aunt, who
put away a little money for us which we used as
seed money to begin my writing career.
☐
And thanks to:
Matthew Baerwalde
Eerdmans Printing Company
and
Chris Mulder
Horizon Color Graphics
and
Steve Reyes
Cover Text Design

I meditate on all Your works, I muse on the works of Your hands. I stretch forth my hands unto You...in You do I trust: cause me to know the way wherein I should walk.

-David-

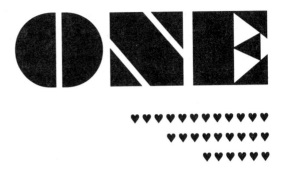

ONE

♥ ♥ ♥ ♥ ♥ ♥ ♥ ♥ ♥ ♥ ♥
♥ ♥ ♥ ♥ ♥ ♥ ♥ ♥ ♥
♥ ♥ ♥ ♥ ♥

The Hardest Puzzles Have No Borders

I was near the end of putting a jigsaw puzzle together. I was at the very slowest portion of the task: those tree top pieces which all look alike. Jim sat down next to me.

While I tediously labored, Jim told of the hardest puzzle on which his family had worked—*to start with, it had no borders.* Thus, they had no clue that any potential border was indeed the outside edge until they were long into putting that entire puzzle together. Among other ingenious novelties this creative puzzle-maker connived into that devious end-product was *five correct-appearing extra pieces which did not go to the puzzle!* "It was the hardest we ever put together," Jim said, "but it was also the most enjoyable." We laughed at the grand prospect of working on such an imaginative creation.

End time Bible prophecy is like that puzzle.

Prophecy can be the hardest riddle in the Scriptures. Still, it can also be the most enjoyable. The Creator of all has added a number of ingenious novelties of His own to make the study of it overwhelming. He added one **significant requirement** which has made it the final of all His doctrines to be cracked.

Prophecy's Long Standing Obstacle

We read about that 'long-standing obstacle' in Daniel's last chapter. That beloved servant of our Lord was told that the End Time verses of his last prophetic vision in the final chapter were *sealed until the 'time of the end.'* Our Puzzle-designer Lord was not going to allow any, even those of His wisest and His most learned discerners of His Word down through the centuries, to understand and to execute the End Time puzzle before its time.

It turns out that what we had thought was the 'outer edge' of the Prophetic Puzzle was not the outer edge at all.

That is so important, let me repeat it.

What we had thought was the outer edge of the Prophetic Puzzle was not the outer edge at all. Some of what we thought were major pieces in the Prophetic Puzzle are not 'pieces' in this puzzle at all.

The Sealed Key Piece

Daniel was given the key piece of the prophetic puzzle in the very end of his book. At the very end. Once it was received and written down *an extraordinary thing happened*.

The Heavenly Messenger who gave that information to him then told him that that key piece was sealed to the time of the end. Other similar 'sealing' statements in the sacred scriptures make it abundantly clear: the words spoken meant *none would understand that key piece until the time of the end.*

None.

That has been prophetic truth, my friends.

None have understood.

None.

All who study the book of Daniel are able to understand the book for the most part. However, when those scholars write on those verses in the last half of the last chapter of his book...they draw a major blank. The rest of Daniel seems easy enough to be comprehended by the various scholars, but one after another all tell us they do not know to what the author Daniel is referring in the last half of chapter twelve. If one does try an attempt, that explanation is usually followed by something like: "and this is as far as any teacher can safely go." *However, as I said above, it is a very key piece to the prophetic puzzle.*

A very key piece.

Especially verses eleven and twelve.

Consider this, most of us truly believe we are now living in the time of the end. Therefore, should not the simplicity of that **HITHERTO SEALED PORTION OF DANIEL'S FINAL CHAPTER NOW BE DISCERNIBLE?**

That was the promise, wasn't it?

That was the Heavenly Messenger's promise to Daniel.

That key piece of God's Game Plan would be sealed only to the 'time of the end.'

Since many believe that we are in the time of the end **then the words are no longer sealed.**

Is That A Bear?

"What's that black thing?" our then four year old daughter inquired after we had moved to Michigan's Upper Peninsula—and we were on our first visit to the far western end of its huge Porcupine Mountain Wilderness State Park.

No one answered Laura.

In fact, none of us took much notice with her question. We were tired from hiking and we just continued eating the cookies we had with us at the picnic table.

She then asked, *"Is that a bear?"*

I did not know if anyone else heard that one. But I did. So very slowly I turned around to look at the spot where she was pointing, and, sure enough, there was a big black bear! And it was close! By the time I had looked...***Bonzo*** was no more than a couple picnic table's length away from us!

Ever so slowly I began to rise.

Keeping an eye on the wild creature—we were new in the area, and we wanted to see a bear, I reminded myself, though not this close—I began to devise a scheme to move my family out of the picture as safely as we could.

When I finally reached full stature...having kept **HIM** in my sight the entire time...I slowly turned to give to the rest of the family my carefully thought out instructions for them to begin moving very slowly back toward the car.

When I was fully turned, to my huge surprise I saw that my wife JoAnn had already grabbed our daughter in one arm and had snatched the bag of cookies in her other hand, and that she was over two thirds the way to the car with them!

Making very good time!

We still laugh about it to this day.

Is That Jesus Christ?

My daughter's questions, "What is that black thing?" and, "Is it a bear?" began it all that day in the park. There's a day coming when someone is going to turn to his neighbor and ask, "What is that white thing in the sky?"

As those around continue to '*eat and drink*,' they are not going to take much notice to that question either. They will go on continuing to eat and drink until the same person asks with more alarm, "Is that Jesus Christ and His warring hosts coming back again to this old earth?"

Who is going to grab what? And to where are they going to run, at that moment?

Who's car is going to help them out at that moment?

Who's going to laugh about it later?

God's Game Plan

That bear had a plan. That bear's goal involved getting to a garbage can very near where we were sitting. Therefore, we discovered in hindsight, that we were not included in his plan. Which discovery we were very thankful about.

God also had a plan.

He still has the same plan.

I call it His 'Game Plan.'

You and I are included in that game plan.

Where we are included will determine the very important answers to those last questions we saw above: who's going to grab what and to where are they going to run at that moment. Indeed when Jesus Christ comes back down to this old planet, where you and I are included in His Game Plan will determine if we will be laughing at all.

Be advised . . . whether we choose to be or not, we are all included in God's Game Plan. In it, He says that He is going to reward the small and the great. Our God also says that He is going to judge the small and the great. None of us is *too small* to miss one of those alternatives. Nor is any of us *too great* to miss one of them. From those small to those great there will be none who will be passed over.

We are all included in God's Game Plan.

What Is A Game Plan

What is a game plan?

A game plan is simply a set of blueprints and strategies, sometimes written sometimes not, decided upon by a coach or any leader as to how he, or she, would like to have their 'team' play in the upcoming game.

Any purposeful scanning of the prophetic teachings of the Bible will show that God has already presented His Game Plan concerning how all of history will proceed, and, concerning how He wants His human creations to play their portion of the game.

Being one-hundred-percent accurate up to the present is the astonishing record that our Lord God has accrued. Nothing has happened in history which has caught our all-knowing God off guard. Nothing in the future will either. And the game—as far as this day of grace in which we are living—is almost over. It seems to be well into the final minutes of the final quarter.

Our God and Creator is accurate! However, not only is He so precisely accurate, He has proven to thousands and millions that He is also such a great Coach for Whom to play. That is if His 'team' (you and I) will offer Him our own one hundred and ten percent!

A Game Plan Is A Battle Plan

Symbolically, in a sporting event the two teams are at war and they are out on the playing field to determine who is the 'victor' and who is the 'conquered'.

Jesus warned: two nations should never go to war with one another unless each one has a game plan conceived which will make victory a very real possibility. Before countries go to war the leaders had better sit down and 'count the cost' of such an endeavor. Sit down, *count the cost,* and make certain that they have a very good fighting chance of winning before they call their men into action.

In His Word, our Lord God has presented His entire Game Plan. However, as we stated above, in His infinite wisdom, He caused one very major piece of that game plan to be sealed (*ie, no way understandable*) until the time of the end.

And as we have also stated.
Since many believe that we are in the time of the end *then the words are no longer sealed.*

A Word Of Caution

One word of caution is necessary though. That key piece of the Prophetic Puzzle changes more of the rest of the End-Times Charts than we would have ever guessed.

Major changes come about when we **ENTER** this key piece into the puzzle.

Many of us will not like these changes.

Many of us will not even accept this new unsealed piece of the prophetic puzzle because we are 'locked' into all that work we did through the years to create and understand our prophetic charts as they presently are.

Like the new wine Jesus came to proclaim, this unsealed key piece to the puzzle also needs a new wine skin. And, like Jesus' message and the kingdom's inception He came to bring about, this new unsealed piece will never make it...if it does not get the needed new 'wine skin chart' it has to have to survive.

Let me repeat the gist of that thought.

Even as our Lord Jesus' new Christianity could not flow out of the old wine skin of Judaism but had to have new 'wine skins' of its own for its new wine...so the biblically 'unsealed' teaching of prophecy has to have the understanding which can only come when Daniel's visions are unsealed. Thus, new wine skin charts are now needed.

The *old wine skin we all have studied* looks somewhat like the chart below:

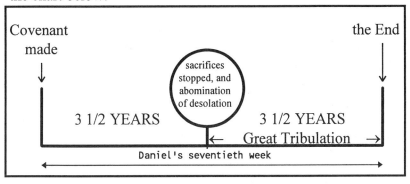

Until this new piece was unsealed by our Lord God for our use, the old wine skin chart we used tried to present everything that was understandable from the prophetic scriptures. That old chart has done a quite commendable job. Certainly, almost all of us accepted it with minor adaptations. *How did we know that its outer edge* (**the End**) *wasn't truly the prophetic puzzle's outer edge?*

Indeed, how did we know that that finish line depicting the End and the second coming of Christ was NOT THE LINE ON WHICH those two events were to occur.

We can choose to be adamant and hard-nosed and childish

in demanding that those wrong pieces ARE for this puzzle. Or we can sit back and laugh at ourselves and accept that the joke was on us. And proceed forward to correctly finish the puzzle.

● The Piece Makes The Puzzle Simpler ●

This present wine skin chart has been with us so long many will not give it up willingly.

Many will not give it up at all.

That's the nature of old familiar wine skins.That's what our Lord Jesus told us about old wine skins.

You agree, do you not?

Nevertheless, our friend Daniel was given a very significant key piece of the prophetic puzzle and was **then** told it would be **unsealed at the end of time**—and, that *those that were wise in* **that generation** *would understand it.* With it, they would better understand the entirety of God's Game Plan all the way to the end. They would see the simplicity of it all. For all puzzles are simple once *the puzzle-doer has perceived how they should be put together.*

Back in the Rubric's Cube rage, did we not thrill to watch those who had mastered that seemingly impossible cubed maze.

The Heavenly Messenger did not say that 'new manuscripts would be mysteriously found' holding the new key piece to the Prophetic Puzzle. (Along this line, as a writer, I was taught that I could <u>not</u> withhold some crucial truth to my unsolved mystery –and then spring it upon the reader right at the end of my novel *when my hero would incredibly find it! And solve the case!* I was thus warned: I could not do that. No 'springing it upon the reader.' Not if I wanted to gain credibility with them.)

It is the same with the Lord.

He will not spring something upon us at the time of the end which we had no clue about beforehand. He will not bring forth a *'new manuscript'* citing new facts to assist us in that quest to understand the End Times.

((That is what is SO wrong with the belief that our Lord has FINALLY allowed us to FIND some *'much better because they are older'* manuscripts of the sacred scriptures. No, my friends, our Lord God would NEVER HIDE HIS PUREST WORD for nearly 1800 years *and then spring it upon us!* Never! Or He is not God. We have always had His purest...those FOUND in the last 150 years are very corrupt. Instead of being the 'BEST' as the newer versions claim, they are among the WORSE.))

He did not say that *'new revelations'* would be given in the time of the end which would present this new key piece of the Prophetic Puzzle.

He did not say that a **'new body of believers'** would burst forth at the time of the end to present this new key piece to the Prophetic Puzzle.

No new manuscripts were to be found.
No new revelations were to be given.
No new body of believers would be bursting forth.

The Heavenly Messenger said those final words that Daniel had written would be sealed until the time of the end. He stated that even though Daniel finally understood the meaning of that end-of-his-book, sixth vision, *none in the long-coming-future would understand it until the time of the end.*

Look at all the books on Daniel.

Read what those books have to say concerning that last half of that last chapter, and, you will find that Heavenly Messenger was one hundred percent correct on that point. All the books on Daniel claim that they are bewildered in their attempts to state just what Daniel was trying to communicate to us in those final verses of his book.

Of the authors who believe the events described are for the future, they basically write three things:

One. The 'time of the end' would conclude with Daniel's 70th week of years: the final period identifying with the last three and a half years of the seven years. See Daniel 12:6-7 where the linened One on the river clearly states that.

Two. There is to be a stopping of the daily sacrifices and the setting up of the 'abomination of desolation' on the same day. After those two events there was only to be three and one half years. Therefore...they have no real clue as to what Daniel 12:11 is referring to, when it confidently instructs us to take those 'two' events as our starting point, and count *three and one half years plus one month.*

Three. Again begin with the 'one day' in the exact middle of the seven year period when the daily sacrifices are stopped and when the abomination is set up — from that day we are to count *three and one half years* **plus two and one half months** and we come to a day when those who "wait for it will be blessed." Why would they be blessed who waited until those two and one half months after the end of Daniel's seventieth week? These authors inform us that there is really no 'good' explanation given.

In a nutshell...the above three points are what we find when we come to almost all books dealing with Daniel...if they try to say anything about the verses in the last half of his last chapter, *and if they believe that chapter is still for the future.*

Take a moment. Do you have any books on Daniel? Turn to Daniel 12:6ff in those books and scan what those authors teach. All that I have studied basically give some variation of what I have just shared above. To be on their side, what else could they have written? What truths could they have gleaned? We read in Daniel 12 that the Heavenly Messenger emphatically informed him that those last verses would be <u>sealed</u> until the time of the end.

That Was A Divine Sealing

Light will not lite upon those words.
Darkness will cover over those words.
It has throughout history.

Those words have been like the *little scroll* in the Father's right hand. None was sufficiency worthy, even John was not, to open or unseal it until Jesus as the Lamb of God came forth and received it from His Father's hand. Our Lord Jesus was worthy back in John's vision and the day is soon coming when He will in actual history again receive that little book from the Father's hand and unseal each of its seven seals.

Then, *only then*, will the words of that little book be ready to be read and understood. Only when it is 'unsealed' by Jesus. What an awesome day that will be!

So it is with much of Daniel's last chapter.

It too **was sealed.**

Sealed by God Himself.

But, it was only sealed 'until' the time of the end. It was to be understood, or opened, or unsealed, at that future time of the end. It was not to be sealed, for example, until Jesus came again for us. It was sealed only until the time of the end.

It Is Therefore No Longer Sealed

So many of us believe we are in the 'time of the end.' Do we not hear believers referring to that fact all the time? Seemingly, day after day.

Thus, that key piece of God's Prophetic Puzzle is no longer sealed or closed to us. The words of Daniel's last chapter are to be understood. That is the promise of the Heavenly Messenger.

   * **There is no 'hocus-pocus' here.**
   * **There is no 'new manuscript' found here.**
   * **There is no 'new revelation' given here.**
   * **There is no 'new group of believers' coming on the scene to show the rest of us this new 'key piece' to the Prophetic Puzzle. There is none of those things.**

There is simply going to be an understanding by those of us who now read it in the 'end of time' in which we are now living.

It will not seem earth-shaking.

It will not move us much, but it will be *understandable*, and *that understanding will burst wide open the entire Prophetic Puzzle.*

Daniel 12:6ff will no longer be sealed.

Up to the time of the end it had been.

That was how our Lord God wanted it to be.

That was how He demanded it to be.

That was why the Messenger said the final information was

to be sealed.

The Unsealed Key Piece

I will now present the unsealed key piece to the Prophetic Puzzle from Daniel twelve. Upon studying that piece, you will notice how our charts will have to be altered by this new key piece.

You will also see how simple it is.

It will not seem earth-shaking.

It will not move you much.

You will probably at first say, *"Ho hum...big deal."*

Still, I'm going to present it.

I will also take those who desire to travel with me through much of prophesy to see how the entire prophetic picture will be more simply understood because this key piece has been opened to us by our Lord.

And I mean it when I say 'to us'.

It is to us **Bible-believing, Jesus-following, blood-bought, Heaven-seeking**, people-of-the-Book who are going to be wise unto all understanding in the time of the end. It–*the unsealing–* will show to us the simple understanding of Daniel 12: 6-13.

Below is the new key piece to the Prophetic Puzzle (God's Game Plan) that our Lord God in His great wisdom sealed right up to the time of the end. The key piece He had **sealed right** up to the time in which we are presently living: right up to the end of the second millennium of this day of grace in which we're in the final moments of living.

```
    *        *        *        *        *        *


DAILY SACR STOPPED ←1290 DAYS→ ABOM OF DESO SET UP

DAILY SACR STOPPED ←1335 DAYS→ BLESSED WHO MAKE IT


    *        *        *        *        *        *
```

That's it, friends.

That's the new understanding.

That's the new unsealed key piece.

I said it was simple.

I said you'd say, "Ho hum...big deal."

Nevertheless...you will see how these two little changes in our charts will amazingly alter what you have always accepted. We have always been instructed to place the two above events–the daily sacrifices being stopped and the gross abomination of desolation being set up–**together** at the very beginning of those two times given.*We agreed to place them in the very beginning because this true simplicity was sealed from our eyes.*We could never have seen it any other way. It was sealed by Heaven...and that was that.

Sunday's Bulletin

If this statement was in this Sunday's bulletin: *'from the time that the VBS props shall be taken away, and the chairs for the evening concert set up, there shall be four hours and thirty-five minutes.'* If that 'not-so-common-way-of-saying-it' was in the bulletin would you have ANY trouble figuring out what it meant?

No. You might wonder why the person stated it that way—but almost anyone reading it would smile and know that 'from the time the Vacational Bible School props were taken away' at, let's say 1:25, Saturday afternoon, that those in charge of the task THEN had *four hours and 35 minutes* (or until 6 p.m.) to have that room cleaned and the chairs set up for that evening's 7 p.m. concert. Thus, the auditorium would have to be 'READY' one hour before the concert was to be put on.

Even so, we are now to read Daniel 12:11-12, in simply the same similar manner: *'From the time that the daily sacrifices are taken away* (that gives the time of the first event) *and the abomination of desolation set up* (that's the time of the second event) *there shall be 1,290 days,* (i.e., BETWEEN the two noted events).*(And from the same time of 'the sacrifices being taken away') blessed is he who waits until 1,335 days* (later).'

Even so, now we can look at those ending verses of Daniel and 'see' what we could not see before. Just as with the Sunday announcement in the bulletin, there are *two sets* of *two events given, and between those two there are specific spans of time.*

One thousand two hundred and ninety days

And one thousand three hundred and thirty five days

Indeed, the first thing we have to see and lock in our minds is that the time periods given in those last verses go **BETWEEN** the two stated events. Thus, the arrows pointing to the events:

```
A  ←   1,290 days   →  B
              and
A  ←   1,335 days   →  C
```

The second thing we will **see** in the new revised chart on the next page: both spans of time mentioned go beyond the final day of Daniel's 70th week, and thus, *they go* <u>beyond</u> *the final three and one half years of that week of years.*

Let me repeat that.

Both spans of time go beyond the final day of Daniel's 70th week, and thus, **beyond** the last three and one half years of that week of years. *Now that the sealing has been removed we can see* that that is precisely what Daniel was shown to be the case in the answer to his deep probing re-asking of that all-important question we find in Daniel 12:6: *How long shall it be to the end of these wonders?* Shortly we'll go to that passage and spend some time in it.

But for now remember the Sunday bulletin criptic: '*from the time that the VBS props shall be taken away, and the chairs for the evening concert set up, there shall be four hours and thirty-five minutes.*'

Yes, if we want to ... we can figure out statements which are stated in a way a little different than we are used to.

> from the time the VBS PROPS shall be taken away,
> and the chairs for the evening concert set up,
> there shall be four hours and thirty-five minutes.
> ⊗   ⊗   ⊗   ⊗
> from the time the daily sacrifices are taken away,
> and the abomination of desolation set up,
> there shall be one thousand two hundred and ninety days.

Pretty simp, eh?

*From the time the props go **'bye-bye'** and the chairs are **set up**, there will be a lapse of four hours and thirty-five minutes.*

Even so, from the time the sacrifices are **'stopped'**...and the abomination is **set up**, *there will be a lapse of 1,290 days.*

And, from the time the sacrifices are **stopped** and those who wait are blessed, *there will be a lapse of 1,335 days.*

Our New Wine Skin Chart

Using this 'unsealed' understanding of Daniel 12:11-12, we now produce our new wine skin chart of the Prophetic Puzzle. You will not believe how solely these two verses can reshape our accepted old wine skin chart. As we say in business these days: *they will take us right off the charts.*

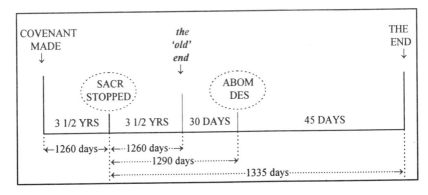

The old border is no longer the border.

The outer edge is no longer the outer edge.

That is *the difference*. What we had always accepted as the outer edge of the puzzle is no longer the outer edge of it.

There are now *two extra time periods* given: a 30 day period, and a 45 days period. And, therefore, some of the other pieces are also drastically changed.

The Great Tribulation Is Much Shorter

Once you see this, you'll love it.

Until you see this, you'll hate it.

Up front, we find that the **great tribulation** is much shorter than we have ever thought it to be. Much, much shorter. On the old wine skin chart it was usually three and one half years long. In the stories and films that are popular it is that long. Three and one half **YEARS** long. However, if this new key piece of God's Game Plan is correct, we find the great tribulation is only forty-five **days** long.

Forty-five **DAYS** long.

DAYS not YEARS.

Think about it.

Could our Lord God Almighty pour out His wrath *for three and one half YEARS*?

Would He?

Could His creation endure such an out-pouring which was *three and one half years long*?

Let me repeat that.

Would our Lord God pour out His wrath for 'three and one half years?' Would He? Could His creation endure such an out-pouring? Remember: *in forty days He killed all living flesh.* **In 40 DAYS** He totally **inundated the ENTIRE earth!** Back then waters 'completely covered the face of the earth' for one hundred and fifty days.

In forty *days* He killed all living flesh.

Up to now we have been instructed to believe that our Lord God in His wrath against the wickedness of the peoples on this planet will pour out vial after vial of destruction for three years and a half!

Friends, do we know what we are claiming?

Do We Really?

Do we really understand the 'Almighty Power' of our Lord God up in Heaven? How could the citizens of this globe endure such a long outpouring–for Jesus promised that the elect would endure–for their sake the days would be shortened.

> Going from *forty days* in His first outpouring of His wrath, to *one thousand two hundred and sixty* (1,260) *days* during His second outpouring of wrath. That does not sound like any kind of 'shortening of the days' to me.

Does it to you?

Going from 40 days all the way up to 1,260 days!
That's a shortening?

How could we have gone so wrong?

We had no choice but to accept that 'long period of days in our previous prophetic teachings.' The old charts gave us those long dates. All the old teachings gave us that ridiculously long period of time.

They basically *forced* us to accept that our Lord God would pour out His wrath for the one thousand two hundred and sixty day period they deemed as the time of the Great Tribulation.

Look again at the final sections of the new wine skin chart.

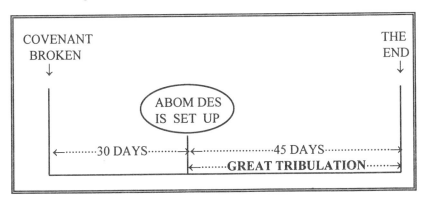

Friends, the Great Tribulation will be **only forty-five days** long. We will see that the 'wrath portion' of the great tribulation will be less than forty days.

> Let me repeat that. *We will see that the wrath portion of the great tribulation will be less than forty days.*

That is very significant.

Our Lord Jesus made that very significant.

For He made it very clear that His Father would shorten the number of the days of wrath-outpouring this time around. That first time our God destroyed all flesh upon the face of the earth in forty days. During this coming time of wrath-outpouring, the number of days will be shortened for the elect's sake.

Jesus told us that.

According to our new wine skin chart **the days will be less *than forty days of wrath***: exactly what Jesus said. Therefore the elect will survive the outpouring!—I say that those days are less than forty because of a future chart we will review in this study soon. That chart will show that the wrath-days of the great tribulation are not more than thirty-five.

> *From forty days* (of the Great Flood) *to thirty-five days* (of the Great Tribulation), *now that is truly, truly, a* **shortening of the days.**

Would you not agree?

From forty (40) days down to thirty-five (35) days.

We find in this new wine skin chart that Daniel's seventieth week is *neither* the Great Tribulation *nor* the Day of the Lord. It has a very significant part to play in the end time, however, for some reason the brimstone fireworks begin one month *after the end of those seven years.*

**Daniel's seventieth week is not the Great Tribulation.
Daniel's seventieth week is not the Day of the Lord.
Daniel's seventieth week is not in the Day of the Lord.**

What Question Did Daniel Re-ask?

Our friend Daniel asked the same question we would have when he heard THIS for the first time.

Turn to Daniel 12:6.

He is listening to a question asked to the Man clothed in linen standing on the river. The question: "How long shall it be to the end of these wonders?"

It was a simple *'when'* question.

A simple *'how long to the end'* question.

How long shall it be to the end of these wonders?

The Man clothed in linen standing on the river answered with fanfare, "It shall be for a time (a year), times (two or more years), and an half (an half year), and when he shall have accomplished to *scatter the power* of the holy people, all these things shall be finished."

Simple answer.

But not to Daniel!

My heart and pride goes out to him when he immediately—impetuously—exclaimed, ***"I heard, but I do not understand! My Lord, WHAT SHALL BE the end of these things?"***

His is not a 'when' question.

His is a simple *'what'* question.

It's a question we ask when we are not quite certain or when we do not understand something.

WHAT Shall Be The End Of These Things?

He is concerned about the 'end of these things.' Not 'when' these things shall end. He was satisfied that these things will end at the end of the three and one half years.

However, he did not understand the END of those things.

The *'what'* that shall be at the end.

And how could he have?

That is why his question is so awesome!

Let's look again at the original answer.

The simple answer of the Man clothed in linen had said that *the coming wicked prince* **would have the power of Daniel's holy people** *scattered. At the end of the three and a half years the power of Israel would have been* <u>scattered</u> *by the wicked coming prince.*

No wonder Daniel heard but did not understand.

How Did His Other Visions End?

Here are the promises he had received in his other visions:

"....in the days of these kings shall the God of heaven set up *a kingdom, which shall never be destroyed....*" 2:44-45. "...the greatness of the kingdom under the whole heaven *shall be given to the people of the saints* of the most High,whose kingdom is an everlasting kingdom...." 7:27. "...(the king of fierce countenance)shall also stand up against the Prince of princes; but **he shall be broken**.." 8:23-25. The whole of 9:24-27 promised the same truths. The fifth vision ends with: "...*your people shall be delivered,* every one that shall be found written in the book."

All his other visions on the time of the end concluded: with **his people reigning in glorious splendor;** with his holy people **controlling an everlasting kingdom** and with the "king of fierce countenance" broken *(not __with the power of__ his __people broken and scattered__); and with his people delivered!*

The very opposite of his people being scattered.

No wonder he did not understand the answer of the Man on the river.

His People Delivered And Reigning, Not Scattered

So he had all those promises of Israel reigning, not of Israel and its sovereign power being scattered at the conclusion of the seventieth week of years. That is why he heard the answer, but *did not understand it.* Therefore he stiffened his back and asked the correct question.

"WHAT SHALL BE THE END OF THESE THINGS?"

It was the perfect question.

He was not chided for asking it.

Still, the Heavenly Messenger didn't change the *what* at all in the new answer He gave. The Messenger, however, changed the *when.* The linened messenger *changed the timing of the conclusion of the seventieth week.*

That is so important!

Let me repeat it: The Messenger changed the **timing** of the conclusion of the seventieth week.

The Messenger Had Not Been Wrong

Daniel thought that the *'what'* of that linened Messenger's answer had been stated wrongly. No. No, the Messenger hadn't made a mistake in His proclamation. Absolutely—the power of Daniel's holy people would be scattered by that coming prince when that final seventieth week came to a conclusion. That was correct. *What Daniel assumed...and what we today in our old wine skin charts assume is that the final day of the seventieth week concluded the visions.*

No, no, no, he was told.

No.

No.

No.

Daniel had done what we do today.

He had cut into the Heavenly Messenger's answer. The Man had proclaimed only the first part of the answer to the question that had been asked in verse 6, "How long shall it be to the end of these wonders?" He had only answered that far—and Daniel cut in and *in bewilderment* cried out that he did not understand the answer that he had been given.

The Heavenly Messenger first told Daniel that he was to go his way and then....

And then....

He finished His original thought.

First, the Man made it certain that many would be purified and made white and tried. He also made it clear that the wicked would continue to do their wickedness. (Why are people today so surprised that wickedness is so widespread and so intense in our world?) The Man also made it clear that none of the wicked —but only wise people—would understand.

Understand what?

His Father's Game Plan.

His Father's Prophetic Puzzle.

The Man clothed in linen standing upon the waters finished His complete answer with this word: "...from the time that the daily sacrifice shall be taken away *(which we have seen was in the exact middle of the seven years of the seventieth week),* & the abomination that maketh desolate set up, *there shall be one thousand two hundred and ninety days.*

"Blessed is he that waits, and comes to the one thousand three hundred and five and thirty days."

Daniel must have felt just like Job at that moment. In 40:4, Job could say nothing else to the Lord but:"What shall I answer You? I will lay mine hand upon my mouth."

I will keep my trap shut next time, Lord.

"Daniel, your holy people *will be scattered at the ending of the three and a half years,* but blessed will be all who wait and *come to the one thousand three hundred and thirty-five days after the stopping of the daily sacrifices."*

Daniel had the answer he wanted.

He had the correct 'what'—and the correct 'when'—to go with it.

The Correct What
And
The Correct When

He knew there had to be a concluding day in which his own people were to be blessed.

He knew there had to be a concluding day in which his own people were to reign over the rest of the earth.

All his other visions had claimed those two things.

I believe he was overjoyed with this answer.

I believe we should be overjoyed with it. For we know that that day is also the glorious day which our Lord Jesus will use to come and set up that everlasting kingdom! It will be that day when we will appear with Him from Heaven!

It just appears, however, that *that day will occur two and a half months AFTER the conclusion of the seventieth week.*

That is not my timing.

That is not my idea.

That is the timing of the Heavenly Messenger.

That is the timing of the "Heavenly Messenger" in the linen Who was standing upon the waters of the river.

The *"certain Man clothed in linen, whose loins were girded with fine gold of Uphaz. His body also was like the beryl, and His face as the appearance of lightning, and His eyes as lamps of fire and His arms and His feet like in color to polished brass and the voice of His words like the voice of a multitude." That, friends, is our Lord Jesus in one of His pre-New Testament appearances in the Old Testament. See Daniel 10:5&6.*

Therefore, the day which will begin the new eternal kingdom of our Lord Jesus will occur *two and a half months after THE CONCLUSION of the seventieth week.*

In God's Game Plan our Lord God wanted His Son to be the Messenger Who would present the timing of when His Own kingdom would be set up.

Those are Jesus' words.

Not mine.

Those are Jesus' timings.

Not mine.

If He wants to inform Daniel that the seventieth week ends with Israel scattered and therefore the 70th week's LAST day is NOT THE CONCLUDING DAY for which we are looking, we would then do well to also accept that truth.

Why should we argue with Him?
Really!
Should we argue with Jesus?
Should we argue with the Truth?

Did not Simon Peter teach us anything about Who will win, and who will lose, if we argue with our Lord Jesus?

Of course, Jesus will win.

He is the Truth.

And He said to our wonderful friend:

"Daniel, your *holy people will be scattered at the ending of the three and a half years,* but blessed will be all who wait *and come to the one thousand three hundred and thirty-five days after the stopping of the daily sacrifices.*"

Let's look again at the new 'wine skin' chart:

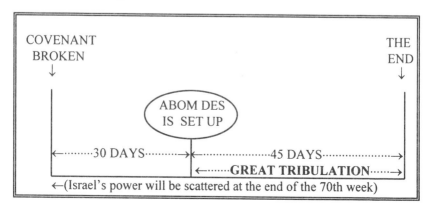

THREE

The Spirit Is Our Teacher

If you have come this far then you know that we are going to have some fun.

If you have come this far then you are thinking some about what I have written. I do not want to *'in moving too fast'* drive you away. However, I detest books that give us readers a superb first couple chapters, and then, fail to give us anything like it in the rest of the pages. I'm certain that you do too.

Surely the Spirit showed us how to write a book. The Bible starts out with such an awesome beginning and continues to get better and better.

What powerful writing!

When things get gloomy for Israel, and all is lost, *then* they come bouncing right back into the land!

And *then* comes the Gospels! The life of Christ is full of so much emotion and power—and, *then* comes His trial and death (what a sad time), BUT, *THEN* comes the resurrection!

Like I said, what powerful writing!

May the Spirit be our Teacher and our Editor.

Ten Days Of Tribulation

In the light that the **'Great Tribulation'** will be forty-five days long and that not all of that suffering-time will hold God's outpouring of wrath upon the earth, look at Revelation 2:10:

> *Fear none of those things which you shall suffer:*
> *behold, the devil shall cast some of you into prison,*
> *that you may be tried; and* **you shall have tribulation**
> **ten days***: be thou faithful unto death and I will give*
> *you a crown of life.*

I hope those six words jumped out at you.

I hope you are saying to yourself, "I've never seen **ten days** *(TEN DAYS)* **of tribulation** in that verse before."

Ten days of tribulation.

TEN DAYS.

Amazing!

This eye-opening truth was given to the church of Smyrna– you know that two of the seven churches were given very good 'report-cards' from our Lord.

An **A-plus** was given to the church in Smyrna.

An **A-plus** was given to the church in Philadelphia.

To this church in Smyrna Jesus said, "I know your works & your tribulation, and poverty (but you are rich)." He carried on to inform them that they would have *'tribulation for ten days.'* During those '**ten days**' they were to suffer, and some of them were to be thrown into prison by Satan...they were to be tried... some of them would be required to be faithful unto death.

For the sake of prophetic understanding, please, accept that this promise of *enduring only ten days of tribulation* is being addressed to the *'still-upon-the-earth'* church in the beginning of the great tribulation.

Please, for the moment, *accept that the church is still here upon the earth when the Great Tribulation begins.*

Many of us have been taught that that simply will never be the case. We've been taught that our Lord would not allow us to experience the harshness and suffering that will come upon the earth at that time.

Many have ridiculed those who teach *that believers will be here when the Great Tribulation begins.* Again let me remind us that the verse we just looked at <u>are the words of Jesus.</u>

<u>They are not my words.</u>

<u>Jesus told an **'A-plus'** church</u> (Smyrna) that their believers would suffer and have tribulation ten days and that some would be cast into prison and be tried, and some would die. That truth is in the book of Revelation. That truth is in the book that deals exclusively with the time of the end.

Ten days of tribulation. Some would be cast into prison. Some would die.

Those are Jesus' words.

The *very same Son of God* Who told Daniel that there was going to be forty-five days of great tribulation. Two & one half months minus one month is forty-five days. Here in Revelation He tells us, as far as the church is concerned, what will occur in the first ten days of the Great Tribulation.

Let us put that key piece into the new wine skin chart of the Prophetic Puzzle:

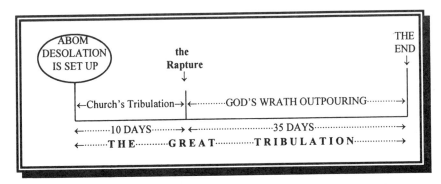

Friends...the *Great Tribulation* is only forty-five days long according to the authority and dictates of our Lord Jesus, and if the church is going to endure ten of those days *as per again* the words of Jesus, then, we should *find* that the RAPTURE of the church occurs AFTER the Great Tribulation begins.

Before we probe for evidence in other biblical passages that the rapture of the bride of Christ will occur after the Tribulation begins, we need to look at the words given to the other *'A-plus'* church in the opening chapters of The Revelation.

Please turn to Revelation 3:10:

"Because you have kept the word of My patience, *I also will keep you from the hour of temptation which shall come upon all the world to try them that dwell upon the face of the earth.*"

There certainly is the possibility here that Jesus will rapture the faithful believers out from that 'wrath-portion' of the Great Tribulation which shall come on all the world to try those "that dwell upon the face of the earth."

Matthew 24:15

Like we said, there is a possibility that Jesus will be coming to take us Christians out from this old world *before* those harsh dark days of the wrath-portion of the Great Tribulation actually begin.

If so, then we should find evidence which presents the long-awaited rapture of the church taking place *after* the Tribulation begins (Rev.2:10) but *before* the outpouring of the wrath of God begins (Rev.3:10).

And we find plenty.

Friends, let's turn to Matthew 24:15, to begin our search for that evidence:

"When you therefore shall see the abomination of desolation spoken of by Daniel the prophet stand in the holy place.... Then let them which be in Judaea flee into the mountains...."

Thirty days **after** the *conclusion of the seventieth week* of

Daniel's vision, **Jesus,** the linened Messenger, **said to Daniel** that the 'abomination of desolation' would be set up.

Here in Matthew 24:15, the abomination of desolation is set up in its desecrating location. It is standing in the holy place.

The Great Tribulation Commences

In Matthew 24:15, that abomination of desolation is seen as set up, and, Jesus warns all over there in Judaea to flee for their lives. He explains the reason for His order in verse 21:

"For then shall be great tribulation, such as was not since the beginning of the world to this time, no, nor ever shall be."

First the abomination of desolation.

Then the Great Tribulation begins.

It is here that we have placed the new piece of the 'ten days of tribulation' that many faithful believers will endure. During those ten days, Jesus commanded us: "then if any man shall say unto you, Lo, *here* is Christ or *there*; believe it not."

Here is why the belief of that rapture in *'mid-heaven'* is so important. Many will come saying, and believing, that our Lord Jesus Christ has returned, and *is here or there on the earth*.

Not in mid-heaven.

'Here' or 'there' on the earth.

And...it could be believable because: "there shall arise false Christs and false prophets...shall show great signs and wonders; insomuch that, if it were possible, they shall deceive the very elect." 24:24.

"Wherefore," Jesus continued in v.26,"if they shall say unto you, 'Behold, He is in the desert;' go not forth;'behold, He is in the secret chambers', believe it not."

The Abomination of Desolation is in place.

The Great Tribulation has begun.

The faithful church is beginning to experience suffering and tribulation from the evil one. It is then our friends & neighbors come claiming that Jesus Himself HAS come, and can be found *'here'* or *'there.'*

"How do you know it is Him?" we ask.

"Oh, you should *see the great signs and awesome wonders he is doing. Surely he is the Christ."*

But the timing is not right.

Nor is the place.

He is to meet us in the clouds.

Not 'here' or 'there' on the earth.

Nor are we to seek Him *out there in the desert* nor *in there in the secret chamber*.

The Rapture As Lightning

"For," as our Lord next claimed in v. 27, *"as the lightning* cometh out of the east and shineth even unto the west; *so shall also the coming of the Son of man be."*

That, friends, sound like an 'in-the-air' rapture to my mind. "As lightning...so shall also the coming of the Son of man be." Do not listen to and follow those that say He is here or there on this old earth. But do watch for our Jesus *to come as quickly as a lightning flash in our heavens.*

Let me repeat:

That, friend, sounds like an in-the-air rapture to my mind. "As lightning...so shall also the coming of the Son of man be." Truly that 'lightning-coming' is the Rapture.

> **The Abomination of Desolation is set up. 24:15.**
> **The Great Tribulation has begun. 24:21**
> **The church experiences "ten days" of suffering & tribulation. Rev. 2:10**
> **False Christs and prophets multiply throughout the earth claiming to be the coming Christ 'here' and 'there'. 24:23-26.**
> **It is then in those days that we are to look up for our redemption draws nigh.**

> **As a mighty "lightning bolt" sizzling through the sky from the east to the west. In such an instant our Lord Jesus will come and snatch us home. 24:27**

In a nutshell: *abomination* (v.15), *tribulation has begun* (v.21), *Christs claim to be here and there* (v.23-26), *church's rapture into the heavens* (v.27), *end of tribulation* (v.29).

Then...**AFTER** the Great Tribulation there is *another great glory-coming of Jesus to this earth.* 24:29ff.

During *that* very-visible, very-slow *coming* all the tribes of the earth shall be able to see our Lord Jesus coming again. That visible-to-all coming will last much longer—much, much longer —than the *lightning-fast east to west coming* presented in verse twenty seven.

One Coming Or Two Comings

Of course that demands two comings. Can we not find 'two comings' in Matthew 24? In verse 27 we read: "...so shall also the *coming* of the Son of man be." And in verse 30 we read that after the tribulation, "...they shall see the Son of man *coming* in the clouds of heaven with great power and great glory."

Luke 17:22, also presents the truth of there being more than one "day" of His coming again. The Gospels do clearly present two comings of Jesus.

Jesus Himself stated **very emphatically** that there would be *more than one coming again by Him to this earth.* He did not state it to the Pharisees or to any of the other Jewish leaders.

He told it to his disciples only.

For only they believed in His **original** two comings.

The Jewish leaders did not believe in Him.

Nor did they in His talk of a second coming.

"Not our Messiah," they shouted at Jesus. "Ours will come and set up His eternal kingdom ALL IN ONE COMING," they very smugly scorned at Him. "Two comings! That proves You are not the Messiah," they chided without mercy.

But did they understand the scriptures?

Did they see that there *were* two *'distinct pictures'* of their coming Messiah?

Did their eyes remain closed to the "suffering One who was prophesied as coming for the sins of their nation?"

"Only one coming!" they claimed.

Our Lord Jesus replied, "Sorry, friends, but the Son of man has to suffer and die and rise again first. *Only then...*can He, on some future day, return to set up His eternal reign."

To this day that belief in only one coming is the main belief which estranges the Christian and the Jewish communities here on our planet.

One 'Second-Coming' Or Two 'Second-Comings'

Today Christians fight over the same question.

Let me repeat that:

Today Christians fight over the same question

Christians readily accept that it was correct to deem, before Jesus corrected the teaching, that the Messiah was only going to come to our earth once, and, during that coming, that He would set up His eternal kingdom. However, when Jesus presented so clearly on Passover night to His disciples that He "had to suffer *first* for the sins of the world *and then* He would come again to set up that everlasting kingdom"...believers in Him accepted that as a very logical and a very scriptural solution to the *'complete Messiah concept'* as presented in the Old Testament.

> **The Messiah was to come to our earth.**
> **The Messiah was to suffer and die.**
> **The Messiah was to reign eternally in Jerusalem.**
> **The Jews claim this has to all be in ONE coming.**
> **Jesus taught it would happen in TWO comings.**

Christians conclude the Jews are incorrect in not being able to **'see'** that the sacred scriptures clearly present two Messiahs, and, therefore, in not being able to see the belief in Jesus and in His solution to the problem: *which is, His telling them that the Messiah has to come TWO separate times. He has to come in Two separate comings to fulfill two different missions.*

Now we come to our Lord Jesus' second coming and lo and behold we have that **same problem** hitting us squarely between the eyes again.

Many Christians believe, like the Jewish community did of the first coming, that there simply isn't any place in the inspired scriptures for TWO second comings.

Many other Christians, reading the same scriptures, believe that there has to be two second comings of the Son of man to fit all the second coming verses in correctly.

Jesus To The Rescue

Lord Jesus came to the rescue in the first dilemma—though the Jewish communities did not embrace His solution that there would actually be TWO comings.

We still pray that those 'natural children of Abraham' will accept His wise teaching on that subject: that their Messiah had to die first...and then, He would come at a second time to set up His eternal kingdom.

Instead, the vast majority of them living today are going to accept ANOTHER who comes in his own name to be their 'one time coming' Messiah. They have wholeheartedly accepted his nation already ... soon, very soon, they will accept him to their utter judgment.

Jesus also taught us believers that there would be more than one second coming. Why do so many believers not accept that teaching of His?

Luke 17:22

Jesus said to His disciples: "The days will come, when you shall desire to see **'ONE of the DAYS'** of the Son of man, and you shall not see it."

I sincerely hope those **FOUR WORDS jumped out at you** in a way you never saw them before.

"You shall desire to see

one of the days

of the Son of man."

That is, the time will someday come in the future when His disciples' suffering and tribulation is going to get so ghastly for them that they are going to greatly desire to see *one* of the *days* of the Son of man. Why didn't He say,"You are going to desire to see My day? Or My coming again?"

Why did He specifically say, "You are going to crave to see *one* of the DAYS *(plural)* of the Son of man."

Why did He pluralize DAYS? *For the same reason He told His disciples that He, as the Messiah, would have to have TWO main comings to fulfill all the scriptures.*

Clearly in the context of Luke 17, ***DAYS*** refer categorically to His 'coming again.' See verses 24, 26, 30, 31 and 32–where 'that night' has the same meaning as 'that day' of v. 31.

Friends, there is coming a time when things are going to be so bad for His followers (i.e., the first ten days of the tribulation) that they are going "to desire for ***ONE* of the COMINGS** of the Son of man."

Yes, we can place "COMINGS" in place of "DAYS" in this context. Our Lord Jesus did:

"For as the lightning...so shall also the Son of man be in his DAY."

First, notice that Jesus claims that the lightning-coming will be *one of His days* in Luke.
Singular.

So shall also the Son of man be in His DAY.

Not: in His DAYS-*plural*.

So this lightning-coming is ONE of His days.

You ask, "How do we know this DAY is referring to one of His COMINGS in the first place?"

Jesus said:

"For as the lightning comes out of the east, and shines even unto the west; so shall also the COMING of the Son of man be." Matthew 24:27.

This **lightning-rapture coming**, friends, is the **ONE of the days** that believers in those first 10 days of the great tribulation are going to be looking for! They aren't going to be looking for the second **ONE of the days** of the Son of man–for that DAY (coming) which will follow the great tribulation. Not believers.

They will not be craving a day that ends the tribulation.

Nor will they be craving to see that coming of His to defeat evil and to set up His kingdom.

Believers have been promised an EARLIER DAY (coming) than that one. They have been promised a *'DAY'* which will escort them out of this world before the wrath of God is poured forth.

Jesus tells us that *DAY* will be the same day that the wrath begins to be poured out.

Friends, there is coming a time when things are going to be so bad for His followers (ie, the first ten days of the tribulation) that they are going "to desire for *ONE of the COMINGS* of the Son of man."

Noah and Lot

Let us do some looking at this Luke passage with a special-eye turned toward the singular and toward the plural renderings by Jesus of DAY and DAYS.

Noah days (or time) first:

"And as it was in the days of Noah, so shall it be also in the days (plural) of the Son of man."

Could we not understand from this that what Jesus is saying is that in BOTH of His days (in the rapture-coming **'and'** in the to-the-earth-coming) that lifestyles will be going on as normal– that citizens across the planet will not be living any differently than they do today...*at BOTH COMINGS*. There is no sense of impending judgment with them at either coming. Even as there is no concern or alarm being shown by any of them *at either of the comings.*

There is a singular day: *"until the DAY that Noah entered into the ark,* and the flood came, and destroyed them all."

That *DAY* is a type of the rapture-day.

That *DAY* is a type of the coming *before* the wrath of God is poured out.

According to our new wine skin prophetic chart, the *'day'* Jesus comes again to take His bride out of this world is the very same 'day' the wrath of God begins to be poured out on the earth.

It was the same in Noah's DAY.

"And Noah went in, and his sons and his wife and his sons' wives with him, into the ark, *because of the waters of the flood."*

Yet Seven Days

Earlier, the Lord God had told him that he still had *"seven days* to get all the animals in the ark."

On the eighth day, he and every member of his immediate family entered the full ark because forty days and nights of rain were to begin that *SAME DAY.* In they went because of the waters of the flood. Not that the rain forced them in ... but because they 'trusted in the word of the Lord God' they went in *believing the rains would definitely begin on that DAY.*

One doesn't spend such a long time constructing so grand a sailing vessel at the command of the Lord...*and then,* disregard His pronouncement that it would indeed begin raining that very day. Noah and his family entered into the ark in total belief.

Even so with the church. We will ascend to our Ark (to our Lord Jesus Himself) and *that 'same day' divine judgment will begin.*

Next, Jesus presents a new comparison for us to ponder. He compares one of His DAYS to Lot's leaving of Sodom:

> "Likewise also as it was in the days (time) of Lot; they did eat, they drank, they bought, sold, they planted, they builded. But the same **day** that Lot went out of Sodom it rained fire and brimstone from heaven, and destroyed... all. Even thus shall it be in the *day* when the Son of man is revealed."

Again, it certainly sounds like a type of the rapture-coming. *In fact, after much study, I put the entire seventeenth chapter of Luke into the **rapture** catagory.*

Would not that make sense?

Luke expressly wrote because *he wanted to be clearer in his writing than Matthew and Mark had been,* as he says:

> "It seemed good to me also, having had perfect understanding of all things from the very first, to write to you in ORDER, most excellent Theophilus,that you might know the certainty of those things where-in you have been instructed."

Luke especially wanted to scribe all the teachings and every event in ORDER. For example, being wise, he searched out Mary and got her personal rendering of the time of the birth of Christ. Even here, he put the *rapture passages* in one place which was kept away from the predominately 'coming to reign' passages three chapters later. Thus all of the DAY verses in Luke 17 are about the Rapture. And in this *rapture-chapter*, he instructs us that Jesus specifically said His followers would desire to see **'ONE' of His days (or comings).** Obviously that day would be the rapture.

Please remember Luke 17:22:

> *Jesus said to His disciples, "The days (***ten of them*** *) will come, when you shall desire to see one of the days (comings) of the Son of man, and you shall not see it."*

From that statement we can note that Jesus surely told them that there would be more than one second coming.

Soon John will be leading us through the Revelation and he will clearly show us in that powerful book *"the two future days or comings of our Lord Jesus."*

They are both there.

And they are both defined very well.

They do "progressive revelation" justice.

For now write it down that those who thought their Messiah would only come one time were wrong. That is, they are wrong according to Jesus.

And Jesus is the Truth.

Those who believe that there is only going to be one second coming are also wrong according to Jesus.

The Flood Compared To The Great Tribulation

Before we leave this chapter, we should recap a little on the relationship of the Great Flood to the Great Tribulation.

First, from Whom came the Flood...and from Whom comes the Great Tribulation. The "great tribulation" comes from either Satan and his men of sin...or, it comes again from the Heavenly Control Center–and thus directly from the Father Himself. It is the contention of this book that the Great Tribulation is a time of dire judgment *again coming directly from Heaven* to judge the evils on earth.

Flood Was Worse Tribulation So Far

The worldwide Flood was *the worse tribulation this planet has seen up to this time.* In the Flood 'all perished', except the eight. That previous greatest of all periods of suffering came *at the direct hand of God Almighty.*

> **In the Great Flood,**
> **at the direct hand of God Almighty,**
> **all upon the earth perished.**

The worldwide Flood killed every living flesh-creature save the few saved from its vengeance within the ark. It was brought on by God Himself.

With that in mind, Jesus says the Great Tribulation is to be the worse time of wrath the world will EVER see.

That time of great trouble must again come from the hand of God. It must come again as an act which He will deplore, but an act He will execute.

He must or His word cannot be trusted.

Jesus continued to say, *"Except the days* (this is a key word: DAYS) *should be shortened, there should 'no flesh be saved'* (this is a key statement: **NO FLESH BE SAVED**): *but, for the elect's sake* (those who endure till the end are going to be saved) *those days* (once again the key word, *days*) *shall be shortened."*

> •1•
> God poured out His wrath in the Great Flood in 40 days.
> •2•
> Jesus said the next outpouring of God's wrath
> will be much, much worse.
> •3•
> But, Jesus also said the DAYS will be SHORTENED.
> •4•
> Think about it.

✦5✦
Much greater the wrath ... but the DAYS shortened.
✦6✦
Friends, the outpouring of God's wrath in the
Great Tribulation will be less than 40 days.

Since the Great Tribulation is only going to be forty-five **45** days long altogether, and, since the church is going to suffer for **ten** of those forty-five days, then for Jesus to say that those days shall be shortened (<u>obviously to less than the **forty day** Flood's outpouring of wrath</u>) begs us to *'see'* that the wrath-portion of that Great Tribulation *will be thirty-five days long at the most.*

The Rains Lasted A Full Forty Days

If the time of the judgmental rains had not lasted forty days, then the Flood would not have destroyed *all flesh* on this earth.

Let me repeat that.

If the time of the judgmental rains had not lasted forty days, then the Flood would not have destroyed ***all flesh*** *on this earth.* If the rains had only been, let's say, thirty-seven days long...the Flood would not have covered the highest stretches of the land *(surely the mountains before the Flood were not nearly as high as the Floodwater-pressure-pushed-up chains of mountains that now can be seen across the world),* and, therefore creatures on those highest plateaus would have survived, and would have lived through the added five months the waters "prevailed upon the face of the earth."

Simply, if the wrath-period of the Flood had not lasted forty days *then all flesh would not have perished.*

Our Lord Jesus speaks of a time of much greater tribulation than that of the Flood. It is a judgmental time that will also destroy all living beings on the earth if the *days are not shortened.* That is, if those coming-tribulation days also last a full forty days then all flesh on the earth would be destroyed again.

But the *days* are going to be shortened!

We have Jesus' word on it!

First, we have His word in Daniel 12 (the Great Tribulation will be *45* days long). Then we also have His word in Matthew 24 that the days are going to be *shortened.* Finally, we have His word in Revelation 2 (true believers in Him will suffer *ten days* of the tribulation...and, therefore, the wrath-portion will only be thirty-five days long.)

Let's look again at the end of our new wine skin chart:

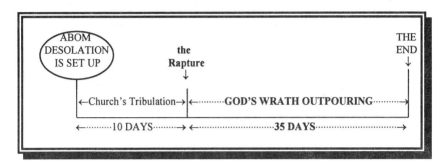

The wrath-portion of the Great Tribulation will be less than forty days long. Our chart clearly shows that. Therefore the days of wrath-outpouring will be *shortened* even as Jesus promised.

So we see the Flood as a TYPE of the Great Tribulation as it most obviously is. In the Flood *all flesh died*. In the accursing wrath-portion of the Great Tribulation...if the days last a full 40 days and are not shortened...all flesh will likewise die.

However, because the 'wrath days' of the Great Tribulation will be *shortened to less than 40 (to 35 days),* the elect ARE going to endure to the end.

*   THE GREAT TRIBULATION DAYS   *
*   ARE GOING TO BE SHORTENED!   *

Shortened to thirty-five days at most.

My Atomic Bomb Dream

I am reminded of a dream I recently had.
It was not a very long dream.

It was of our atomic bomb exploding on the Japanese island and city in the Pacific.

Customarily when we ponder on that tremendous explosion we visualize the rising huge column of smoke—topped off with a gigantic mushroom. Those huge billows of smoke growing & growing higher and higher in our view!

In the dream I was watching the monstrous explosion at the city's ground level. What I saw was the instantaneous bursting out in all directions of the titanic tidal waves of expanding heat and destruction. *In that dream, I was being pushed barely ahead of the rushing devastation!*

Speeding along *backwards* just ahead of the rushing waves, I was watching the immediate despair of the citizens of the city as the rocket-fast, fire-and-brimstone wave incinerated all them without even an instant chance to try to escape.

The tidal wave went on and on, seemingly forever.

It was a literal lake of fire.

And I woke up.

The Spirit asked me in my spirit, *do your people look upon that atomic explosion as hideous? As the act of a demagogue? As the most unmerciful act a country could expend toward an enemy?*

My answer was immediate.

No, they don't.

Though many of us were not around when it happened...no, we Americans do not believe it was an act of a demagogue. We believe it was a merciful act–for it stopped a much larger World War. We are extremely sad that it had to occur, but we believe that since it did have to, that we were righteous in our dropping it on them to show them our lusty strength with the explosion... and, we have not ever had to employ such a device again in any of our wars. (Of course, there were two bombs that we dropped in all at that time.)

In the years that have followed, we have proven that we are not demagogues. A vile dictator would use, and reuse, such an explosive power to demand total subservience of all the nations of the world. We have not.

After I answered, **the Lord reminded me that He also has explosive fire and brimstone and a lake of fire in His 'Game Plan' against His enemy.**

He reminded me that it too is very destructive. That it's used only as a last resort also, but that it will be activated against His enemy.

As I lay there the thought that came next was:

> *How does your American nation look upon Me because I have said that I have fire and brimstone and also a lake of fire that I am going to make use of 'to also put to the end' the extremely long war I have had with the one you call Lucifer and Satan?*
>
> *Is your American nation as forgiving of Me as* **they are of themselves** *for having such a powerful explosive in my 'Game Plan' to bring to an end an exceedingly destructive war which has gone on for millennia?*

Do they see my 'lake of fire' as a merciful action? Or as an unmerciful one?

One final question: do your Americans believe I am right or wrong in using such a destructive way to stop My war with My enemy?

I thought again of the atomic bomb in my dream:—*massive tidal waves of flames and volcanic destruction radiating out equally in every direction without any advance warning to an entire city and island of fateful citizens. Tidal waves that were of such immense proportions they engulfed every living-soul within their ever-widening, ever-enlarging circle in a fire and brimstone lake of fire!*

The WWII cease-fire was almost immediately called for.

That was our 'only reason for creating' that flaming lake of fire: to cause the enemy to cease their wicked aggression which we had deemed inhuman and wrong.

I lay there and knew what I was to write.

Friends, our Lord is no less unmerciful.

Our Lord has no delight in using His lake of fire. He has no delight in using fire and brimstone in His final battle of this age with His enemy.Still,He has already placed in His word that He is going to use such powerful, destructive, explosive forces–for the very same reasons that we used our versions of them: that is because His enemy will never cease his aggression against Him and His righteous peoples all over the face of the planet;unless, in an act of extreme mercy, our Holy Lord God causes him and his followers to experience what our Lord's wrath is really like.

Our Lord is going to use those forces.

But the days will be shortened!

This time. Shortened to less than the Flood's forty days–for the elect's sake!

Review Of The Shortened Days

The Bible says God poured out His wrath for forty days and nights with the results that all flesh on the face of the earth died in the great Flood. To this day we have telling signs all over the scarred face of our planet that the ravishing pressure and power of the worldwide Flood caused an horrendous destruction to the once fertile outercrust, the entire land surface, of our planet...and a violent eruption of vast ranges of mountains.

You know that Jesus tells us that His Father will again pour out His wrath with greater vehemence than He exercised in that first time. He tells us that the days will be shortened (obviously to less than the original forty days)so that all flesh doesn't once again perish off the face of the earth as they did in the Flood.

Therefore it needs to be noted:

**The Great Tribulation is not
Daniel's Seventieth Week, nor half of it.
God will not pour out His wrath for seven years,
nor for three and a half years**

FOUR

Speak To Us, John

Outwardly my stay on the island of Patmos appeared to be a drag, penned the apostle John in the first century of this era. I was exiled over here for my preaching and teaching of our slain and risen-again Jesus Christ of Nazareth.

I was old, and tired, and discouraged.

Life had been so good when our Lord Jesus was with us.He taught so wonderfully, and we all thought that He was going to set up His Earthly Kingdom. That was back then. Since then...it has been rough.

Especially these last few years.

At first, when the Spirit came and fell upon us it was just as if Jesus had never left us. Instead of He, it was **"we"** who were doing all the miraculous acts. We really missed Him greatly but we all believed that He was coming back right away "to take us to be with Him."

Then, as each of His closest followers died as martyrs over the decades, we missed Him even more. And...we realized that, for some reason only known to Him, He was not going to come again for awhile.

Then I was sent over here. The days, the weeks and months have moved very slowly. It has been very hard. I knew I would never return to the mainland.

Nor would I ever return to my calling.

I was getting too old. My only real reason for being around was that I was one of the few who was still alive who had been with our Lord Jesus. That fact was enough to get me an entrance and a hearing within any church gathering.

John's New Cross

Before I came over here of course.

Here was my new cross.

I would bear it. I would . . . no matter how hard it would be upon my aging body to be over here in exile.

Like I said, I would bear it.

Everyone of our group of disciples who personally loved & knew our Lord Jesus, and who had seen what He went through for us, would bear whatever we had to for Him.

Therefore day after day after day, I bore the bad happenings which had fallen upon me for my being true to God's Word and for my testimony for our Lord and Savior Jesus Christ.

I was not getting younger–for all I knew, I could well have been the final of the twelve to still be alive.All the reports I had heard were hard to accept,though our beloved Lord had warned us: most of His disciple-friends had died by martyrdom.

Here I sat day after day after day facing that same troubling fate in banishment myself. *It was not just my hard condition, however, that was bothering me*—there are so many antichrists out there trying to deceive, and deceiving, the churches.

Over here I did not know what I could do to stop them.

I surely could not vacate this isle and show them the truth.

Enter The Spirit

Then, praise God! One glorious day it all changed!

One glorious day **His Spirit** entered my cold confinements and took me like Ezekiel of old!

It was great!

It was wonderful!

And you will never believe where He took me!

He took me in the spirit to **that Day** in which He will come to our rescue. The Lord's Spirit took me to 'that Day' in which He will destroy those which are destroying this world. He took me to *that Day* when He shall reign with all His glory and with all His might.

His Spirit took me into the Lord's Day!

He took me into the 'Day of the Lord,' my friends!

Friends, there I was shown all the details of the 'Day of the Lord!'

I still cannot believe it!

In that personal encounter with the Spirit, He led me away like Elijah of old!

It was great!

It was wonderful!

Write, John, Write

And ... you will never believe that, at my very old age, our precious Lord Jesus, through His Spirit, has commissioned me to do a lot of writing for Him!

I mean a lot!

I have written, and written, and written, and written and the words just keep flowing and flowing and flowing! Now I am on my first writing of this book you are reading. And the events of that wonderful 'Day of the Lord' are coming back to me as if it happened within the last few hours!

The last few minutes!

Even as I write—*I think: friends, I was taken into the time that all our followers of our Lord Jesus have wanted to know more about since the day He was taken from us. And...I was even taken by the Spirit right into Heaven!*

Into the midst of Heaven itself!

It was the Day of the Lord!

The Lord's Day was just beginning!

Isaiah has written about it. Zechariah, and others in the Old Covenant, have told us further things about **THAT DAY**. Paul has written and talked often about it. And, now, here in solitude on this isle of Patmos, in the spirit, I have also entered *that Day of the Lord!*

I have been over here writing ever since!

This is the **third set** of scrolls I have worked on since I beheld all those wondrous scenes. The first book I wrote, and the words just flowed off my hands. I mean, the events, and quotes, and thoughts just came back so vividly into my mind that I could scarcely do anything else but write.

Write.

Write.

Write.

Of course, at a time like that when everything is flowing so well, *I had no desire—or want—to do anything else but write, write, write.* I do not know how long Matthew, Mark, or Luke took in compiling and writing their stirring stories of the birth, life, death and resurrection of our Lord Jesus—but I know that when I began to obey our Lord's command to write of '**those things which we have seen,**' I know, friends, that those words came without ceasing for moment after moment, and for hour after hour after hour. *In His plan I was in the perfect place to obey His command to 'write of those things' which we twelve disciples had seen.*

I was here in solitude in exile!

And I wrote.

And wrote.

And wrote.

And I finished that wonderful story of our Lord knowing all the time that I was writing so that each, and every, reader could 'know' that they had eternal life! The real eternal life I had just got through seeing and experiencing up there in Heaven myself ...I entered Heaven a number of times during my traveling with the Spirit. I have seen all the beauties of that future magnificent Home for all of us who will live forever and ever and ever with our Lord and Savior Jesus.

Therefore I had a *Heaven-inspired, definite reason* to write about in my gospel which neither Matthew, Mark nor Luke had when I sat writing of 'those things which I had seen.'

I hope that it blesses everyone who reads it. I did not try to follow the other three Gospels. I desired mine to be different, to simply present Jesus as He truly is—*the Son of God who came down from Heaven into our world to show us His Father and to tell us how we can live with both of Them forever!*

Once I concluded that long telling I have obeyed our Lord's command to next write about 'those things which are.'

Those Things Which Will Come To Pass

I have just finished writing an 'epistle' which will be taken to as many churches of our Lord Jesus as can be. All I need is to get it back to my church in Ephesus and then they can take it along with this scroll of my Gospel to all the churches in the world:for the time must surely be short til all these things come to pass!

Having obeyed our Lord in writing of *those things which I had seen,* and, of *those things which are in the here and now,* presently I have come to the point of writing down those things *which I have seen which will come to pass.*

Even as His Spirit reminded me of so much as I wrote those first two scrolls, I sense His Spirit's ever-presence with me as I remember and write: the scenes, and the events and the persons are filling my mind's eye with such clear views.

So now, concerning what I have seen which will soon come to pass: at first I had thought that I had actually entered into the Day of the Lord in all reality! That I was there in my body and forever. Soon I realized I was only there in the spirit.

The events up there went on and on.

On and on.

Therefore this last book is also going to become a very long scroll. Of course *the Day*, like *any day* to our Almighty Creator and Father, is **'as a thousand years of our timing.'** So in our reckoning as I passed often between Heaven and Earth, I was involved (especially nearer the end of the visions) in being in the spirit for quite a long time. *Though it did not take much of our time in actuality—probably just one afternoon.*

Why he chose me to be the one to see all that I do not know but I am ever so grateful that He chose me.

Bear With Me, Friends

Three score years ago we disciples had been able to live on this Earth here with Him for nearly four years...and now He has allowed me to be with Him all this further time to 'preview' the coming events which will lead up to, and, which will complete, the *mystery of our Father* up through that *soon coming Lord's Day* which I have just experienced in the spirit.

Please bear with me.I will share with you all I went through of those most ominous one thousand years.

Bear with me...for all we disciples realized that Jesus, while with us, gave us greater and greater knowledge, and greater and greater understanding, to the teachings which had their **'kernels'** started back in the books of Moses or elsewhere in those books of the Old Covenant.

My Hour Is Come

To this day, I can remember Jesus telling us those ominous words: My hour is come.

What meaning was packed into those four words: *"My hour is come."* He had said those to us when we thought that He was on the verge of the very opposite meaning than He meant when He had spoken. We were certain it would be the most esteemed year He would have, for it would be the year He would SET UP His throne in Jerusalem: therefore, at the time I confess we had no idea what He was talking about.

Absolutely no idea.

"Let not your hearts be troubled," He began.

Unbelievable!

We had believed that He and we were on the very threshold of *the greatest years of our being together*, and, He says, "Let not your hearts be troubled." My friend, before He said that our hearts were anything but troubled!

Mine became a little troubled at that point. Then He told us that He was going to soon leave us and that was why we should not let our hearts to be troubled!

Unbelievable!

We did not want to believe Him.

We did not want Him to ever leave us.

But how could we not believe Him?

Then He went on and on describing in much fuller detail all that He came to our world to accomplish and all that was going to happen to Him to cause greater accomplishments to come to pass. Then He told us of 'Another Comforter' whom He would send to take His place among us.

In truth that night we would have much rather had Him just talk of all the millions of things He had accomplished, and, that Jesus would have told of all the millions of things He would be doing in the coming years. But, Jesus dwelt that entire evening and well into the night on those things which *we did not covet Him to be voicing.* Things which were hard to hear.

Friends, our hearts *became* troubled.

Still, our inner beings knew that Jesus had shared so much more with us that evening about what we call the good news than was ever shared to any of us before. And, of course, concerning His death and resurrection, He told us so many new details than we ever knew.

Progressive Revelation Is What We All Need

Tell us the 'kernel' of something brand new. Then add more and more through other men and books. *And then*, hit us big in the end if that is what He wants to do...and, that was what Jesus wanted to do!

Friends, that is what He did concerning His death.

Oh, did He tell us!

After His resurrection, and after His Spirit was poured upon us, then *we remembered all that He had shared with us* and we were able to realize that His death was His doing! His hanging on the cross was not the doing of our Jewish leaders, nor that of the Roman leaders.Our Lord Jesus died because our Lord Jesus allowed them to kill Him.

Therefore, because His sacrificial dying on the cross for our sins was His own doing,He made it abundantly clear to all of us what the prophets and servants had made known in a much less full way. But, even then, it took His Spirit's inward teaching to fully make known to us what He had shared on that last night with Him.

He died because it was the will of His Father.

Well, when you finish reading this scroll that I am writing then you will see that He has presented to me, John, a lot more than we have received up to this time concerning His coming again.

So much more.

Unbelievably so much more.

Wait until the middle of this book when I start writing on all that He has shared with me on the famed 'Home-taking' of anyone and everyone who is a follower of His. I have lots to share on that glorious event!

This scroll will end up being as long as the one I have just written concerning His life and death and resurrection. He has shown me so much to write about concerning the Day of the Lord. Now I have no question as to why I was exiled over here so late in my life. Our Lord Jesus has chosen to do the same for me as He did way back then on that Passover evening when He told us so much about His soon-coming death. Once you finish reading what I am putting down, you will see that everything about our future has been already planned out long before it will ever happen. I now know that the primary purpose I came over here is *to be in solitude* so I could enter into the Day of the Lord ... and *then have enough solitude* so that I could write down all the words that He wants me to write.

And to think that I was nearing the end of my life, and that I had experienced so much, and that I had never written down for any of our many churches one word of all that I had gone through with Him and His followers.

No wonder brother Paul spent so many years in bonds. Our Jesus wanted to be certain that he would distribute to the various churches all that he was being shown concerning our peoples' sacred scriptures. I now know that he was in those bonds because he would need the time and the solitude to write down all that he was learning and teaching.

I have penned a long scroll on His life and death, a shorter but pretty long epistle to instruct the churches today (I began both of them in nearly the same way. Once I was in Heaven so many times, I just had to begin both scrolls with the impressive wonder of Who this One truly was Whom we had seen and had held and from Whom we had heard the words of life!), and now I am writing this last scroll concerning all the new revelations of Him, of our Lord Jesus Christ.

First the '**kernel**' of His coming again was given way back then to us when He promised that He would come again to take us to be with Him *"that where He was, we should be also."* Then the many newer visions to add to the truth of that kernel. Finally this revelation of Jesus and of the Day of the Lord! It is truly wonderful: He has revealed so much new revelation to me now that I near the end of my life.

I am so thankful and honored that He chose to use me to bring forth this huge pouring out of new visions. His Spirit used Peter and Paul so often in their writings and preaching to bring forth new grandiose 'revelations' for the teachings of our faith. He has now chosen me to see these new wondrous things, and He has distinctly commanded me to write all these things down.

The Lord's Day

Immediately I was in the Day of the Lord. It is the day when our Lord God is going to say even as Jesus said so long ago to us twelve, "My hour is come! This is the time in history when I am going to take back from My enemy the complete control of this world I have created for My pleasure and for My created ones."

Since Jesus has called me His 'Beloved', and since He has shown me so many scenes concerning that FINAL DAY in His Game Plan for this old world we live in, I like to personalize it by simply calling it 'HIS DAY.'

It is our Lord's Day. HIS DAY when He once again is in total control.

Thus, I intimately call the Day of the Lord: *the Lord's Day.*

It has a ring to it, does it not?

The Lord's Day.

It is a future thousand-year-long Day.

All I want to do when I write this book...*all I want*...is to be fully obedient to our wonderful Lord Jesus and obedient to His threefold command to me.

Write.

Write.

Write.

The first two writings are done.

My gospel and then my epistle, I have them here with me even as now I am beginning to write this last one.

Throughout our holy scriptures *the Lord's Day* is the time during which our Heavenly Father takes over complete control of all the events which occur upon this earth.

It is the Day when He and He alone reigns over our present earth. In all, that Day will last one thousand years according to what I have been shown.

Peter was shown the same thing.

He was told that a *'DAY'* to our Heavenly Father is *as one thousand of OUR years.* He therefore wrote, "But, beloved, be not ignorant of this one thing, that one day is with the Lord as a thousand (of our) years. *And a thousand years is as one day."*

Then he immediately continued, "The Day of the Lord will come as a thief in the night (Paul had already told us that, that is how it all begins and Peter goes right on to tell us how the

Lord's Day *thousand years* will end) in the which the heavens shall pass away with a great noise, and the elements shall melt with fervent heat, the earth also, and, the works that are therein shall be burned up."

Peter also saw that the Lord's Day would continue right up to the coming of a new heaven and a new earth.

The Spirit Took Me Into That Day

I first heard and saw Jesus.

First and foremost! I saw our Lord!

Oh, it had been so long.

Too long. I thought I would never see Him again until I had died.

What a deep voice He had!

What burning eyes!

He looked so powerful!

So overcoming!

I saw Him in all of His wondrous glory, power and beauty! And I saw Him like that in the midst of seven churches which I was told represented all His body everywhere in the world! Just to see him again! It was marvelous!

He was *'standing in all His majestic beauty'* even as our brother Stephen saw Him standing on the day he was stoned to death! Stephen saw Him standing on the right hand of our God and Father in all His glory!

In my vision, even as the **Lord's Day begins**, He, as the mighty One, had left the Father's side, and, He had taken *His rightful place standing in our midst!*

In the midst of all the churches! The awesome Lord's DAY was beginning, and THERE He stood in our midst to protect us and to provide for us! What a sovereign Master we serve!

I fell down dead in His presence! I HAD NO CHOICE!

He immediately revived me, stood me up, and said to me, "I too was dead once. But *no longer*, and *now I am in control of death!* Beloved John, I am here to personally instruct you to write three accounts to My body of believers.

"The first is a historical book of all you disciples have seen of My life with you upon the earth. The second book, a letter of encouragement to My churches. And finally, a book containing all that I am about to show you concerning the final days of this portion of time here on the earth."

I can tell you, *I want to tell you*...my seeing Jesus in His all wonderful, awesome might and beauty has aided me to write the history of his earthly life and my letter of encouragement to our ill-hurting churches (as I said before, I began each book almost the same way because of all that I have just seen in the spirit. Because I have seen Him in all His glory and in His 'Home-setting,' I have begun those books from the perspective that His life and ministry truly began long, long, long, before those days back there in the stable in Bethlehem!)

My book on the Revelation of Jesus Christ is the fulfillment of the last of the three commands given to me in that opening scene which I had with Jesus while I was in the spirit. This is the book covering all those events *which shall be hereafter*. As far as I know this is the only book written exclusively for all the churches which exclusively handles only the thousand year time period called the Day of the Lord, or as you know I now intimately call THE LORD'S DAY.

(Of course...nowhere in the Bible is Sunday ever called the Lord's Day. Sunday is always the 'first day of the week' or the 'morrow after the Sabbath.'

And of course this one-time use of the term, the Lord's Day, would, under any other circumstances, ONLY be seen as WHAT it is: a possessive term meaning the Day of the Lord.)

> *The book of John*
> *or John's book*
> *One and the same*
>
> *The Day of the Lord*
> *or the Lord's Day*
> *One and the same*

The Day Of The Lord

Let's digress for a moment.

You and I need to understand that a day to our God and our Father, is always one thousand of our years.

Always.

One thousand of our years.

A day from His perspective is a thousand of our years.

The Lord's Day is thus one thousand years long. According to John in the Revelation and according to Peter in his second epistle we find both making it abundantly clear that *the Lord's Day* is one thousand years long. Rev. 20:3-7 and II Pet.3:8-10.

Even So The DAYS Of Creation

The *'days' of creation* were in *our Lord God's reckoning*; *that is, the DAYS were each one thousand years long.* Oh, we all understand that our Almighty could have spoken and:

presto!—
everything was here!

I understand that belief.

I do not believe it for one moment.

Here's why: *it does great damage to our concept of God as our 'Creator'.*

That *He-Spoke-The-Worlds-Into-Being* belief carried to its logical conclusion does not allow our Creator God His majestic probability of creating throughout all eternity.

Let me repeat that:

That belief carried to its logical conclusion does not allow our Creator God His exalted, majestic probability of creating throughout all eternity.

With that *He-Only-Spoke-The-Worlds-Into-Being* belief we are being duped into taking **Godness** away from our Lord God.

"The··heavens··declare··the··glory··of··God," wrote one Hebrew young lad who looked up into them and saw the grand creating ability and the vast eons of many trillions and billions of years that His God had used to create throughout all eternity.

However, consider this. What do too many of our Christian teachers teach us now?

God yawned, and said, "Ho hum," and, with a wink of the eye and with the word of His mouth, **(He touched the side of His nose and),...Presto!** all that empty space was FILLED with all those vast universes and galaxies.

Just like that!

He spoke on the fourth day.

Santa Claus all over again.

No real creative act by a 'Creator'.

Just a word of His mouth.

And, possibly even more importantly, *no physical creating having been done until around 6,000 years ago!*

That, friends, is what happens when our doctrines **'form our beliefs'** in the scriptures.

According to that doctrine, our 'Creator' is not really THE CREATOR. He is just a great 'Orator'.

A 'Creator' would spend His eternity creating.

But not this God some of our 'experts' have made up. This new God of theirs did not create ANYTHING until a mere SIX THOUSAND years ago.

Isn't anyone going to ask them, "What has our Creator God been doing for all those trillions...and billions...and zillions and zillions of years?"

Have you ever asked yourself?

Truly.

Have you ever asked yourself?

Friends, what has our God been doing for all eternity, if He was not creating the vast universes, etc.?

We can stare up at the skies on any clear night...and see that our Creator has been at it for trillions, and billions, and zillions of zillions of zillions of years and, *because of that one fact*, we wholeheartedly agree with our young shepherd friend, David: **those HEAVENS DO DECLARE THE GLORY OF GOD!**

These same 'experts' tell us that we have to believe in a '24 hour day' of creation. Once again, in their belief...God does not create. He just speaks, and Presto!—all is here in that teaching. These orators tell us that our Creating God was doing nothing more than being a great Orator.

All He did was *speak* the worlds into being.

The adherents of that 24 hour day belief tell us, for example, that our Almighty Creator created all the stars on the fourth day of creation. That is, *just six thousand years ago or so,* God was supposed to have produced all the stars and all the galaxies and all the universes. If that was true...then what had He been doing for the eons of eons of eons of eons of eons of time periods for all eternity before six thousand years ago?

The Psalmist said the heavens declare the Glory of God.

They do! *If...if* they show that for all eternity He has been a Creator doing what He likes to do best!

Creating for all eternity.

We have such ample evidence in our star-studded sky every night that we have an Almighty, Eternal Creator! Are we going to let 'some expert' take that all away by teaching to us that we have to believe and claim that our Lord God didn't create ANY STAR until just six thousand years ago?

Certainly, Genesis One says, "and God created the stars" on the fourth day. Obviously Moses was not talking about the vast galaxies and those far-flung universes which inundate evening skies all over our globe & continue out far beyond the distances ever seen by man or his telescopes. Obviously...Moses was not writing about the stars in the night skies which were compared in number to the sand which covers the beaches of the world.

Here Look At This

On the sixth day our Creator-God brought forth all "beasts of the earth after their kind and the cattle after their kind, and everything that creepeth upon the earth after his kind." Did He *speak* them into existence? Are we not told through Moses that He formed each beast *out of the ground* (I believe that our Lord God personally designed and fashioned each one separately and over a period of hundreds of years.)

Let's assume that the '24-hour' theory is correct. Let's also accept that He spoke and PRESTO! All the beasts of the world were visible in a flash! In a *hocus-pocus-nanosecond* they were all instantaneously formed 'out of the ground!' As they ask me, "Don't you believe our Almighty God can SPEAK and it all be right there?"

Of course I believe He could.

I just don't believe that He did.

And...yes...I do like the humorous sign I have seen on some stickers which goes something like this:

> ## I believe in the big bang theory,
> ## God spoke, and <<BANG>>, all appeared.

It gets a chuckle out of me.

I just don't believe it.

I don't believe in either 'big bang' theory.

I believe they both *belittle* our God.

I truly believe that our Heavenly Father & His Son are, and have been, **CREATORS** and that *it has been Their nature to create for all eternity.* FOR ALL ETERNITY. And that all we humans have to do is open our eyes at night and we can preview a large portion of all that *They have been creating throughout the eons **of eons** of eons **of eons** of eons **of eons** of eons **of eons** of eons **of eons** of eons **of eons** of eons **of eons** of eons **of eons** of eons **of eons** of years.*

Also I just do not believe that Moses gives us ANY mystic-laded picture at all. He tells us that the Lord God *formed the beasts* "*out of the ground*" just as He, later in that SAME day, created Adam "out of the dust of the earth."

**Our Lord God formed the beasts
out of the ground.
Our Lord God created man
out of the dust of the earth.**

It certainly seems that there is more than just speaking here.

But, if that is what happened, He SPOKE and *hocus-pocus* the beast were spontaneously there...then our Lord God makes Adam on that same sixth day of creation. Again we read *"that the Lord* formed *Adam of the* dust of the ground", and then He "*breathed into his nostrils the breath of life.*"

Do you really see 'hocus-pocus' again here?

Do you really see Presto!—and there's Adam. One second he is not there and the next he is?

Instead do you not have eyes which *'see'* our God actually **forming** man with all the wonderful, intricate workings which our scientists, and our doctors, and theologians have marveled about ever since?

If He created Adam over a 'somewhat lengthy' timespan–didn't He also CREATE *every beast of the field* in that SAME, PRECISE manner?

And all those various forms of cattle?

Didn't He form each animal with the same precise desire to have each organ and appendage work EXACTLY FOR THE REASON that member was placed there?

He prides Himself in His creations, does He not?

I find Him taking PRIDE in His CREATIONS often in the scriptures I have dedicated my life to.

Should He not?

So very often when He is taking pride He adds, "—*when I* SPOKE *you into being,*" or "—*when I* SPOKE this or that creature *into being.*" *Our Lord God revels in His ability to SPEAK into being His great creations.*

He does?

He never says that, does He?

When our Lord God is taking PRIDE in His CREATIONS He almost always makes a reference to *when He <u>MADE</u> them.*

What Else Has To Happen In That Sixth Day?

What else happened?

Well, let us put it this way. Adam, *on the first day he was in existence on this planet,* had to have done a real lot of *hocus-pocusing* himself!—if the '24 hour-day' theory is believed.

For on that SAME day, our Lord God put him in a prepared garden which he tended and then our Lord God brought him all the beasts He spoke into being; and said to Adam, "Name each one of these animals for me!"

"NAME EACH ONE, ADAM!"

Adam's mind must have raced. I mean, he–Adam–couldn't just '*speak and WHAM BAM it was all done*' like our Lord God could have done. Adam had to see each animal, and, if we are going to be true at all to the intent of this passage, think of a name which would particularly fit that animal.

Now, according to our '24 hour-day' friends, Adam had to be finished pretty fast...*for*...*for* that is not all that happened on that sixth day. Our Lord God had to let him see that in all these beasts and living creatures he was 'purposely' naming, *that he was with real consideration naming,* that there was not among ANY of them a helpmeet for himself.

No helpmeet.

Adam had to purposefully name them all and had to realize that there was indeed no helpmeet for him.

Therefore in that 'same sixth day' our Lord God put Adam into a deep sleep and took one of his ribs, and created a perfect partner for Him. In that *same sixth day*, Adam has to come to and see this one whom the Lord brings to him.

Maybe it was pitch dark by then and that is why he thought she was such a gift! Just kidding, Ladies!

Friends, let us simply accept the teachings of the scriptures. To our Lord one day is as a thousand years. It is much easier & I believe much more scriptural to just let the one thousand year period fit in where *a thousand year period* should logically go. The Lord told Moses that the first evening and morning was the first **day**. Moses obviously wasn't there to call that evening and morning a day.

God called it a 'day'.

And to Him a day is as a thousand of our years.

We would be wiser to understand that all that was created and done on the sixth day happened during a full 'one thousand year period.'

EVERY DAY of creation was 'one thousand years long.' It needs to be if we are going to let God be the 'Creator' that His Holy Word claims that He is. If we want just a 'hocus-pocus', WHAM BAM God then I guess a '24 hour-day' belief might work. That is, *if Adam was a superhuman maniac* in his ability to tend the garden and then to name all those animals the Lord brought to him in it!

The Evening And The Morning

Friends, an evening and a morning does not constitute a '24 hour day,' does it? It simply does not. Where's the *noon time* and *afternoon* in this supposed day?

Generally an evening and a morning make up (let us give 6 p.m. for the evening starting point & 11:59 a.m.for the morning ending point) approximately 18 hour max. An *evening and a morning* make up 18 hours max. Some times of the year maybe three or four hours less. Or fourteen to fifteen hours max.

'Evening and morning' do not have a *'daytime'*.

No *evening* and *morning* constitute a 24 hour day. Not now. Not back then. God did not call those time periods **'night and day'** as He could have if He truly wanted to make us think of a FULL day. He specifically called then 'evening and morning.'

Evening and morning constitutes **darkness and light.** For on that first evening (when all was darkness)...our God created light in that sphere of space (where only darkness resided) and so that creation brought forth a 'morning' *(lightness),* and our Lord God saw that it was 'good'. ***Then, He divided that light from the darkness and named the resulting* darkness and lightness:** *evening and morning*. Nothing to do with our sun nor with the 24 hour rotation of the earth (which was not even 'an earth' at that moment, and, of course, there wasn't a sun at that moment in the creating process either).

That concept, that evening and morning to our Lord meant the 'leaving of darkness or of voidness' to end up with the very exhilarating 'presence of lightness or of somethingness' can be seen in each DAY of creation.

> ***From no earth—to there being a massive sphere.***
> ***From no fowls to fly—to an earth full of them.***
> ***And so on.***

Our 'experts' have in one statement and in one word taken away our Lord God's greatness in creating by telling us that He never even created in the first place (creating as we know what the word means),instead they piously teach us He simply spoke and Presto!—ALL we can see today WAS THERE.

So...on 'Day One' we had no earth and we had no sun and yet we are told by the experts that that first day was '24 hours' long.

Do you remember what all had to happen when we looked at the '24-hour' sixth day.

That's an eye-opener!

Here's Another One

On the fourth DAY, God created the sun. What a marvel— what a spectacular 'creation' for the purpose for which it was created. God also created the moon...what a blessing that lesser light is to us...and how helpful for what He had planned for it in all the future feasts for His children of Israel. (Everyone of their traveling feasts and holidays revolved around the time of the full moon so they could 'see' in the evening in their travels and in their camps.)

He also *made the stars* on that fourth day.

Since this was just a few thousand years ago. I believe what Moses meant when he wrote *stars* was *planets*. To you and me, and to all throughout history, including Moses, the planets that we see up there look exactly like stars. We even call them that. The *morning star* is a planet. The *evening star* is a planet. The *red star* is a planet.

The creation of Genesis One seems to be the creation of our solar system. God and His Son had created universes, galaxies, and other solar systems for all of eternity. Then, came the day that the Two of Them would create the earth and its heavens to be the dwelling place for their next greatest creation: all sorts of living creatures and especially human beings. Genesis One tells us of that creation.

Let me repeat that.

The creation of Genesis One seems to be the creation of only our solar system. God and His Son had created universes, galaxies, and other solar systems for all of eternity. Then, came the day that the Two of Them would create the earth and its heavens to be the dwelling place for their next greatest creation: all sorts of living creatures and especially human beings. Genesis One tells us of that creation.

The Creation Of Our Solar System

It tells us of the creation of our earth and of its heavens...of the creation of our solar system: of our Earth and its sun and its moon, and of the rest of the planets which we see of course as stars. It tells of the preparing of the Earth for life. It tells of the creation of all the various lifeforms which were to inhabit that Earth. The opening scene in the Word of God concludes with the creation of man...and of woman.

The creation of Genesis One seems to be the creation of our solar system only. It tells us nothing of the vast eons of ages of creating those innumerable multitude of creations which fill the ever-increasing reaches of space. Genesis One informs us only of the beginning of the creation of our solar system which was to be brought forth so you and I and all humans could inhabit it and explore its wonders. As well as all living creatures.

I believe that in that creating our God and His Son together made use of a full thousand year period for each and every one of their divisions of creating which They called 'Days'.

Adam Died In One Day

If They called those periods 'DAYS' then they meant one thousand of our years, for that is what a day is to Them.

Did not the Lord God tell Adam that in the 'DAY' he ate of the fruit of the tree that he would die. Did Adam not die in ONE of God's days?

Did not Adam die before he reached 1000 years old?

Yes, I also believe he died spiritually the *instant* he ate of the fruit of the tree.

But he also died *physically*.

And I believe in the 'DAY' he ate of that fruit.

Did he live to be over one thousand years old?

No, though in God's mercy he came close!

Adam, and all humans, **died before they hit** one **thousand years of age.** *Adam was 930 years old when he died.* Nine hundred and thirty years old! Thus, Adam died **in the same day** that he ate the fruit of the tree. As our Lord God declared he would and as God renders a day.

The oldest man, Methuselah, also lived less than a **DAY** in God's reckoning. He died when he was 969 years old.

Have you not asked yourselves why our Lord let man live

as long as he did in the beginning?

It was His mercy, pure and simple.

Our Bible tell us that to our Lord a 'day' is as a thousand years.

Even Noah, from the Pre-flood era lived almost a FULL DAY. He died at the ripe old age of 950! Six hundred years before the Flood and 350 after!

Let's simply believe it.

For those of you who want to hang onto the 24-hour day for the timing of each created period—how do you understand God when He makes claims like Proverbs 8:22-30, and Job 38:4-37, and Job 39:1-30, and Job 40:15-41:34...and all the rest of those passages *which imply that all Their creating processes were very intricate, very complicated, very devised, and were acts which the Son took quite awhile to do.*

Like:

> "Of old has Thou LAID the foundation of the earth; and the heavens are the WORKS of Thy HANDS." Ps. 102:25.

What was Isaiah talking about when he says of our Lord:

> "Who hath measured the waters in the hollow of His hand, and meted out heaven with the span, and comprehended the dust of the earth in a measure and weighed the the mountains in scales, and the hills in a balance?" 40:12.

Or, of the future:

> "...when the poor and needy seek water, and there is none and their tongue faileth for thirst, I, the LORD, will hear them, I the God of Israel will not forsake them. I will open rivers in high places and fountains in the midst of the valleys: I will make the wilderness a pool of water and the dry land springs of water. I will plant in the wilderness the cedar,the shittah tree, and the myrtle and the oil tree; I will set in the desert the fir tree, and the pine, and the box tree

> together; that they may see, and know, and consider, and understand together that the HAND of the LORD has done this and the Holy One of Israel has created it." 41:17-20.

Or:

> " ... saith God the LORD, He that created the heavens and STRETCHED them out;He that SPREAD FORTH the earth, and that which cometh out of it...." 42:5.

Or:

> "Woe unto him that striveth with his MAKER! Shall the clay say to him that FASHIONED it, What MAKETH thou?or thy work, HE HATH NO HANDS? Woe unto him that says...What hast thou BROUGHT FORTH?Thus saith the LORD,the Holy One of Israel,and his MAKER...I have MADE the earth and CREATED man upon it;I,EVEN MY HANDS, have STRETCHED out the heavens..." 45:9-12.

Or:

> "...the LORD that created the heavens; God Himself that FORMED the earth and MADE it; He hath established it,He created it not in vain, He FORMED it to be inhabited: I am the LORD; and there is none else." 45:18.

Or:

> "I am He;I am the first,I also am the last.Mine HAND also hath LAID the foundation of the earth and My RIGHT HAND hath SPANNED the heavens...." 48:12-13. (51:13).

Or:

> "...the Word was God. The same was in the beginning with God. All things were MADE by Him and without Him was not any thing MADE that was MADE." John 1:1-3.

| John 14:3 |

I guess we really cannot leave this thought until we look at John 14:3: "...I go and prepare a place for you." You and I both know what most of these teachers of the 24-hour day say about His preparing our new Home for us.

Do they not say something like:

> **"Friends, He's been at it for nearly two thousand years, what a fantastic Home that is going to be!"**

Can we have it both ways?

Can we really?

Can we claim that our Lord God created (er...SPOKE) the earth into existence with a simple word of His mouth when He prepared it for us as a place on which we would live...*but that NOW He is actually preparing us a place.*

And that our Father and our Lord Jesus have been at it for 2000 years! For two full days in Their reckoning.

Can these teachers NOW CLAIM that He is not just simply AGAIN SPEAKING and WHAM BAM!, HOCUS-POCUS!, ABER-CAZAM! it's already completed two minutes after He arrived in Heaven.

No, friends, these teachers are finally right: He indeed went away to PREPARE us a PLACE which according to the twenty first chapter of Revelation is not anywhere as large as this earth and the rest of the solar system which God first prepared for us (and, which took Them six DAYS—6000 YEARS—to create). These teachers are finally right: Our Father and His Son, our Brother Jesus, are PREPARING us another PLACE and that PLACE has already taken Them TWO DAYS!

It has already taken Them 2000 YEARS!

They've been at it for nearly TWO DAYS, friends!

For nearly two thousand years!

THEY'VE BEEN PREPARING FOR NEARLY 2000 YEARS!

What a glorious Home that is going to be! What else would we expect from Them.

As the saying goes:

They're the Greatest!

Why A Totally New Look At The Rapture And The Great Tribulation?

You do not have to read far enough into any of the Pre-trib, Mid-trib, and Post-trib study books, and you will find each one makes very good arguments against each of the other positions. All seem to have, ***and indeed do have***, major flaws inherent in them to which even their own teachers and books do not offer answers convincing enough. Therefore we have been felt led to offer this totally new teaching because of that one now-unsealed very important scripture in Daniel's last chapter.

That one passage which Daniel was told would be sealed till the time of the end. And which we accept as no longer sealed because we believe we have entered into the time of the end.

You realize all other doctrines can be helpfully studied by going back through church history and through the volumes in our vast libraries—and searching out what men of God taught throughout the ages on the subject.

When we approach the *Prophetic Puzzle*, however, the simple-to-understand wisdom of the final portion of Daniel's vision has been 'sealed so tight' that even the great learned students of God's Word throughout the numerous ages would never be able to see and understand its simple message.

Our Own Calling

In the 70s, the Spirit of our Lord moved us (we are a white family) into a black section of Grand Rapids, Michigan, with one goal: we were to befriend all our new neighbors. We were to show our Afro-American neighbors that a white family who 'obeys the Lord' would gladly be their friend ... and would also gladly take interest in what interested them.

That was our calling pure and simple.

We weren't to set up some church.

We weren't to get attached with any Christian organization working in the area.

Our calling was to simply be friendly and neighborly to a group of fellow humans whom many of our own race were not that too willing to befriend and accept as neighbors. Our move into the city was shortly after the famous race riots which raged and burned in many of the larger cities in our nation in the late 1960s, including Grand Rapids.

We moved into the epicenter of the Grand Rapids riots.

As other whites had moved out of these neighborhoods by the scores and hundreds, we were to move in.

It was a definite calling.

One we obeyed: we had thought and planned that we would always live there at 408 Adams Street S.E. A condemned house became our home, and small yard, and decent size garden for a dozen years.

A dozen years in which we lived in poverty far greater than any of our neighbors for we never accepted any governmental handout or assistance and I worked only part time so I could *be there* where my calling was.

That was our calling.

We were very poor but you would never know it by our modest house, or by our car (though it was a small VW Rabbit with over 200,000 miles on it), or, by our bountiful vegetable garden. Many of our neighbors called it the Garden of Eden.

We just didn't have access to money.

Money-wise we were poor.

But we knew that would be the case when we quit our full time job to move into the innercity. We went in at our Lord's command and on His promise that we could pray to our Father for 'our daily bread.'

We did.

And He supplied.

Though not usually much past our 'daily-bread' need.

And often at 11:59!

I Thrived In The Pre-Trib Teachings

It was there in GR in those dozen years in those conditions which many of our race would not have accepted that our Holy Spirit starting teaching me prophecy from the scriptures.

I had always had an interest in Biblical prophecy since the very moment I accepted our Lord's forgiveness and was saved at a Bible camp as a high school student going into the tenth grade. At Camp Barakel in Fairview, Michigan. I soon became involved with a Baptist church.

Our pastor taught the wonders of the Pre-trib position every Wednesday evening for two years. I never missed a meeting.

I ate it up!

I loved it!

I went to a Baptist college. There I continued to flourish in the delightful act of studying the 'Pre-trib' position of Biblical Prophecy!

I totally accepted it.

The Baptist college gave me five more years of the only 'trib' position I ever thought was biblical. I didn't just take the classes, I thrived in them! I loved the pre-trib position as much, if not more than, any lover of the position today.

After college I continued right on studying and holding and teaching that position.

When *'The Late Great Planet Earth'* was published, I was beside myself with joy: I so agreed with it. I knew so much of what it taught that I thought I could have written it!

Nemesis Questions

Then...then...at work I was challenged by a Baptist friend who had switched to the Post-trib position. I reasoned: *he never could have put much interest in the Pre-trib position ... or Jim would have never made that change.*

I went home with a few questions he had set out. I went home determined to destroy his position and knew it would be easy. I went home determined to show him that the 'Pre-trib' position had NO inconsistencies.

Now, his questions were the ones that our pastors, our teachers and our professors never got around to bringing up. His questions were the ones I had never run across in any of my many hours and years of diligent study.

His questions were the ones which were the 'nemesis' of our position.

His questions deflated my abounding joy.

His questions made me look at the scriptures, and shake my head, and wonder why our Lord God ever allowed those verses to ever be in there!

But they were there.

And I have always believed that we believers-of-the-Word have to always deal with every last single one of the scriptures in complete truth.

So I quickly grabbed my many, many, volumes of Pre-trib books and started scanning through them to find their answers to the dilemma. They would come to my rescue.

Searching as much as I could, I found that *all* of my books skipped over those troubling passages.

Skipped right over them!

I couldn't believe it!

I really couldn't believe it.

So I consulted the many pages of *lists of Bible references* provided in the indexes, and lo, those troubling verses were not even among the references which were listed!

Disappointed, but not totally done for. (I was not going to be hampered by what I found lacking in my Pre-trib books.) I decided then and there that I would restudy the Bible ITSELF and prove that the Pre-trib position was one hundred percent accurate and that there were not any passages of scriptures which would disagree with it!

So I began the study.

I would be honest to every verse.

I would close my eyes to none.

The Months Became Years

The hours become days.

The days became weeks.

The weeks became months.

The months became years.

And...and, and I was no longer a Pre-trib believer, however, our Spirit continued to give me an unfathomable desire to hunt and search the prophetic scriptures.

The years became three, four, five.

Then six.

Then seven.

(Remember, I was 'lost' down in an innercity neighborhood in Grand Rapids. Like John on the isle of Patmos, I was in the ideal location and situation *to get buried in the study* to which I had dedicated myself.)

For seven years I **searched and researched** the prophetic scriptures **alone**. I read and reread those prophetic scriptures without the assistance of any other teaching book on prophecy and without the help of any commentary.

During those years I had *decided to trust only* our Eminent Teachers, our Lord's Holy Spirit, and to trust in the grandeur of all books of wisdom, the Holy Bible itself!

And I limited myself to one Bible version only.

I did not want to become the chooser of which version I was going to use for which passages. I know most all do it, I was not going to. Either ONE Bible had the correct answer, or answers, *or we had no* Standard *to live by was my thinking. It still is my thinking.*

I searched and drew charts.

Read more and re-charted those charts.

I searched the Bible more and found even those latest charts *wanting*.

We were dwelling in that innercity of Grand Rapids' near southeast side. Our calling was to befriend our Afro-American neighbors. It was an outward calling which made my internal drive to search the scriptures all the more possible.

Read on.

I'm not sure how it came about but for the twelve years we lived there in GR we never had a phone (and we have never have had a TV since we were married in 1962, and we also did not take a newspaper or magazine). Therefore...without any of those time-takers and interrupters...when I say that I studied the prophetic scriptures on an average of 'well over' forty to fifty hours a week during those years; I did!

Why Did It Take So Long

Why did it take me so long?

I was pre-programmed to the Pre-trib position and ... I hung onto every bit of every inch of that cherished position as I drew my charts.

I hung on tenaciously.

When another beloved facet had to go by the wayside ... it was hard to let it go. Very hard.

It was extremely hard to let it go.

However, since my only goal was to let the *truth of the Bible* be my one and only final truth, when another one of my position's 'truths' was found wanting after much study I had to let it go.

The second reason I took so long in the study was that, when I was finally convinced that my 'Pre-trib' position could no longer stand up to a full scrutiny, then I felt the 'Post-trib' position was the only alternative. So...I tried to make it work... however, having long been a 'Pre-tribber', I already knew its weaknesses and so it didn't take as long to discard the Post-trib as my position for knowing what the Holy Scriptures say about the end time.

The mid-trib position went even faster.

At that point in the late 1970s, Daniel began to open up! I mean, the blinds began to drop away! The time of the unsealing had come. I knew what our Lord Jesus was talking about when He said that we were to have eyes for the very singular purpose of seeing. So many, having eyes, saw not.

I worked and studied more and more.

Just me.

(Few of our former neighbors and church friends ever came to visit us in our new innercity neighborhood.)

Just me in my little backroom basement solitude.

The New Wine Skins Were Complete!

Finally the day came when I felt that all the scripture in the Old and New Testaments had been *'rightfully placed'* in all my charts. All of them!

I knew I had done the equivalent of a doctor's degree—and I even had my doctor's thesis written!

A brand new position with charts and all.

At that point I decided to go back to my books, and see if any of them would do 'damage' to my position. One by one, I searched through them and found not even one argument raised which would do harm to my charts and position.

Here again is that resulting new wine skin chart:

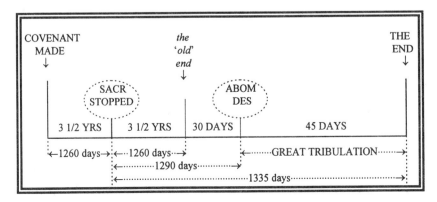

A Long Fight Ahead

In the early 80s, I tried to share my findings with many of my friends and others whom I did not personally know.

I learned that I had a long fight ahead of me.

Even as I was reluctant to leave 'my' cherished position and, even as I fought every new concept that came to me in my study, so it would be true with all others.

I understood the reluctance...*but now I had a 'brand new' position for them to look at.* Still, I was a new kid on the block. What right did I have to present a new position to these learned people. With a disappointed heart, I accepted that the time was not right to try to move ahead anymore with sharing it.

The new Wine Skin chart was put on the shelf. It has been more than a fifteen years since I let my research sit there.

In that time I have studied **writing** on my own, and I have written a historical novel on King Hezekiah entitled: *Now that Forever Has Ended.* Also I have a subsequent novel over half finished. All in an attempt to get somewhat established in the writing field so that when the time came for me '*to try and get these charts and teachings out'*...that I would be able to do so.

I believe the time has come.

We know what religious people did to our Lord back when He walked the earth. (When all He did was show them where they had left the correct path.) Not all of today's Bible-believing religious people are gentle and open to knowing what the Bible has to say on a subject. *It had better not disagree with some of these believers' position!*

I just want to suggest to any and all who will listen that there may be a better and closer-to-the-truth stance to believe in now that Daniel's last chapter has become 'unsealed'.

My friend, the understanding of prophetic scripture is much simpler than we have been taught.

Much, much simpler.

Much simpler.

Progressive Revelation

Please try to grasp this section.

It is so important.

It does not take much in the area of 'brains' to see that the present 'trib' positions all come up lacking when we look at the rapture of the church in the book of The Revelation in the light of the belief called 'progressive revelation.'

Bible truths are often presented with the **kernel** of the truth first given somewhere in the Old or New Testament scriptures. For example, the **kernel** of the good news of Jesus' sacrificial death was presented way back in Genesis.

In Genesis 3:15.

And in *'type'* in our Lord God's shedding blood to make a skin-covering for the fallen Adam and Eve.

First...we are given the opening thought, then...as we read through the Bible, the facts becomes clearer and clearer, fuller and fuller, till the final week of His life when Jesus specifically told His disciples that 'His hour had come.' Then we are given an overwhelming, play-by-play, vividly moving accounting of all the events which occurred up to His sacrificial crucifixion—and those events which went beyond.

That is called *progressive revelation*.

The truth of our Jesus coming back to this earth to take us home with Him also began with a **kernel**. The final statement, which should be as complete as the one we found in the above presentation of the Gospels, we should verily expect to find in the book of Revelation since it's whole purpose is to present to the churches the final revelation of their Lord and Savior Jesus Christ, and to give a final, concluding look at all the End Time events which will finalize this age of grace in which we are living.

(Friend, we really do have to shut our eyes to an awful lot of passages if we are going to try to believe that 'this final New Testament book' was written to the nation of Israel...and not to the church.)

The Gospels dealt with the life, death, and resurrection of our Lord Jesus Christ. Would we not expect to find the most clear and poignant statement concerning His sacrificial death in those four books on His life? That of course is exactly what we discover when we read them. The most 'complete' presentation was not even written until A.D.90 or later when John wrote his Gospel. We have all those words which Jesus spoke during and after the last supper with His disciples only because John, in his banishment on the isle of Patmos, was specifically commanded by our Lord to write his Gospel to go along with those earlier written ones of Matthew, Mark and Luke.

Specifically commanded by Jesus Himself.
No wonder we so love the Gospel of John.

Possibly the 'closest' disciple to our Lord, John had never written down a word about all he had seen, and had heard, and had experienced concerning Jesus. Never. Then in one 'three-parted' command, he was ordered to write about it all—what a treasure of works we have in our sacred scriptures because he was obedient to that one command we find in Revelation 1:19. We are ever grateful to John for his obedience in doing what he was then commanded.

The Revelation is the 'most complete prophetic book in the New Testament' and therefore we would also expect to find in it the clearest and most complete presentation of the glorious future day when our Lord Jesus comes back down to fulfill the promise which was given in kernel-form in John's book in 14:3 where Jesus promised *that once He had 'prepared a place' for them that He would 'come again for them' so that they could always be where He was.*

Clearest Presentation Of The Rapture

> The truth is that, even as it should, the book of Revelation does give to all who study its pages the most clear and the most complete presentation of that glorious day of our going to meet Him in the air!

The unfortunate irony in all this is that the key positions of the time of Jesus' coming again being taught today present to us the very opposite teaching.

Friends, that is sad.

Do not we hold to the belief of progressive revelation in almost all the other doctrines which are so vital to our faith?

Then WHY do we accept any of these three 'trib' positions when not one of them gives us a clear and more complete view of our Lord Jesus Christ's coming again for us at the end of this age?

We find that the 'Pre-trib' position is the very worse in this aspect: for it tells us this *'phantom-truth'* concerning our Lord's returning for us and our returning to Heaven with Him. Turn to Revelation 4:1, they instruct us, and there you will find the Rapture.

THERE we will find the Rapture?

What a joke!

What we read there, if it is indeed the 'Rapture' as they claim, is the *__regression__ of the doctrine, __not a progression__*. (A voice says to John, *"Come up hither."* And John, representing the rising church–we are informed by them–goes up hither.)

And that's it, friends!

THAT'S IT!

Unbelievable!

For the whole entire book!

I thought the Rapture was a **mystery** to the writers of the Old Testament...not to the writers of the New.

We do not actually 'see the church being gathered' to our Lord and Savior. We do not hear any trumpet sound. We do not even see the risen church in Heaven gathered before the throne of God singing and praising Him with all their might.

"Come up hither, John." **THAT is the Rapture?** And yet I believed it for years.

Doesn't say anything, does it?

We know far more about our Lord Jesus' coming back for us in that first proclamation in John 14:3 than we do in this supposedly final Rapture verse. We know much more about the glorious Rapture from the writings of Paul and Peter than we are able to learn from this so very short 'alleged' passage.

> If we truly believe in *'progressive revelation'* then we had better look farther into the book of Revelation for some 'clearer and more complete' passage or passages in this most vital of all the prophetic books of our Bible.

Ties For Last

The equally poor Mid-trib position *'ties for last'* with the Pre-trib position in being the very worse in presenting views of progressive revelation...for it has the former's same ambiguous problem. It tells us to turn to Rev. 11:12. There two witnesses are ordered to, "Come up hither." We are to embrace that those two represent the church! As with the Pre-tribbers, in neither case do we actually see the church being gathered to our Lord and Savior. In neither case do we hear any trumpet sound. In neither case do we watch the risen church in Heaven gathered before the throne of God singing and praising Him with their might.

We also read in the Mid-trib verse,"...and they (the two) ascended..to heaven in a cloud and their enemies beheld them." A portion of the progressive revelation information given in the epistles concerning 'the coming of our Lord Jesus for us' is that His coming for us will occur in the twinkling of an eye. Will our enemies really be able to behold our Homegoing then?

I truly do not think so.

The 'Post-trib' position does not 'present' a Rapture in the book of Revelation either. Their position is that the church will be raptured up to our Lord Jesus even as He descends back to the earth during His second coming. Therefore the Rapture is a *preamble* part of the coming to establish His rule. The two (the Rapture and the Second Coming) are one and the same event.

If that is true, the book of Revelation should have given us *'that presentation.'* What we find in chapter nineteen ... is the leaving of Jesus from Heaven on His glorious white horse. As He descends toward the Earth there is no picture and no clue of the church ever coming to meet Him in midair. No picture. No clue. None whatsoever. *If that was the correct 'timing' for the Rapture then right there in chapter nineteen would have been a wonderful setting to show the 'raptured church' rising to meet Him on His beautiful white steed.*

But, alas, no such presentation is given.

That position also fails a 'progressive revelation' testing of its doctrine.

The New Pre-Wrath Position

The newer 'Pre-wrath' position also does not 'present' any 'picture of the Rapture,' though its teachers do attempt to show the **effect** of the Rapture. Quoting Rev.7:9-17, the Pre-Wrath position claims that those described are the raptured church up in Heaven before the throne. Still, if they are the 'risen church' then why was there no passage/revelation given concerning the cause and the way of their getting to Heaven? Again, a clearer and more complete presentation of our Rapture/Homecoming is not given by this much newer trib position. Those who they say represent the risen church are *just there*!

In this reflection of the book of Revelation that you are now holding in your hands you will be pleased to find **many plump passages** describing *convincing-further-details* of our Lord's coming for us which will vividly present the final clearer and more complete presentation of the Rapture totally in accordance with all the Rapture scriptures presented up to The Revelation.

If we truly believe in progressive revelation then that is just what we would expect to find in any position that claims to present a true picture of the time of the end.

What Should We Expect To Find

Concerning the Rapture, Paul has written that it would take place (1) in a moment, (2) in the twinkling of an eye, (3) and at the *last trumpet*. He told us that it would occur when our Lord Jesus descends from Heaven with a shout, with the voice of the archangel, and with the trumpet of God...and that the raptured ones would be 'caught up together' in the clouds to meet Him in the air.

We should at least expect to find these above details in our Rapture passages in Revelation.

Concerning that day and hour, Jesus said *that no man, no angel, nor He Himself knew when it would occur: that only His Father knew the exact moment of the rapture: the day and the hour.* That should also be pictured.

In 'progressive revealing' we have all this data we can enter into our ever-growing picture of the Rapture. Friend, we should find all this and more in the book of Revelation.

All this and more.

We should.

And we will!

Let me repeat that: *and we will!*

Back To Letting John Tell Us Of His Visions

My End Time prophetic scroll starts with a promise: Blessed is *he that reads* and *they that hear* the words of this prophecy and *keep those things* which are written therein. That promise came to me straight from the Lord Himself.

It also begins with an edifying salutation: Grace be to you and peace from Him which is, and which was, and which is to come (ie, the Father),& from the seven Spirits which are before

His throne; and from Jesus Christ,...the faithful witness, and the first begotten of the dead & the prince of the kings of the earth. Unto Him that loved us & washed us from our sins in His own blood, and has made us kings & priests unto God & His Father; to Him be glory and dominion for ever and ever. Amen!

And a proclamation of His soon coming again: Behold, He comes with clouds; and every eye shall see Him, and they also which pierced Him...all kindreds of the earth shall wail because of Him.

And a word from our Lord God: I am Alpha and Omega, the beginning and the ending.

As The Book Begins
The Day Of The Lord Begins

With those important statements out of the way, I begin my treatise of the *'things which shall be hereafter'*: I, John, your brother and companion in tribulation...being in Patmos for the word of God and for the testimony of Jesus Christ. I was in the Spirit in the Lord's Day and I heard behind me a great voice as of a trumpet. As the Day of the Lord began I turned to see Who spoke with me.

Before me seven big golden candlesticks represented seven churches (which represented every church in the world) and in the midst of the seven I saw One like the Son of man!

His eyes were as flames of fire!

His feet were as if they were burned in a furnace!

His voice was as the sound of many waters!

His countenance was as the brightest 'highest' sun shining in its strength!

When I saw Him, I fell at His feet as dead. He laid His hand on me and said, "Fear not, I am the first and the last. I am He that lives and was dead. Behold I am alive forever! Amen! And I have the keys of Hades and Death!"

Can you top that for a great beginning to a book on the End Times? Do we not all wonder how harsh that time will be when the Lord's Day begins? Do we not wonder how many of us will have to suffer greatly? Do we not wonder how many of us will die. Do we not wonder if we will even miss going through that tribulation altogether.

Jesus told me, "I died and I am now living again! Now I am going to live forever! *If you fear death* I now have the keys of death. *I now can and will personally take you out of death when you enter its chambers.*"

He continued, "Write the things which you have seen." *I obeyed that command with the writing of my Gospel.* (John wrote his Gospel around 90 A.D. The other three were written long before that...probably back in the 50s and 60s. *John did not pen his until he was given this direct command to do so near the end of his life.*)

I was next directed to write *of the things which are*. I this obeyed by writing my epistle (which was written late in his life also. *If our Lord had not commanded him, our scriptures would be without his Gospel, his three letters, and the book of Revelation.* We would be greatly 'lacking in knowledge' of our eternal life, and of the preexistence, and, of the former glory, of Jesus.) And then, of course, I was directed to write this scroll of the things which shall be hereafter.

Seven Precisely Aimed Messages

Jesus next dictated seven precisely aimed letters which I am to send to seven existing churches. These letters are also to be included in this book because every church in every age will need to hear these pointed words of warning.

These seven messages are pertinent for churches in my day, and for those existing throughout the day of grace, but they are especially for those Christians living when the Lord's Day (the Day of the Lord) begins. All believers will need to take heed to these words of our Lord Jesus Christ:

*. I do hold your angels in My hand. I walk in the midst of you, so do not fear. At the same time, do not get so tied up on

your religious activities and spiritual pride that you forget Me. *Love for Me has to 'once again' become 'top priority' in your lives. Seriously...you must rekindle your first love or I will no longer empower you. Then of course you will dry up as a living spiritual body.)*

*. Do not get Me wrong. I do want your loyal works. I do want you to suffer trials and apparent wants for Me. When that is truly performed for Me and not only for show then you are blessed indeed. People do not understand it at all, but THEN you are rich (though you are seen as poor). *Understand this: life will become worse just before I return to get you. For you will experience TEN DAYS of extreme tribulation* which will cause everything up to then to seem mild and to have been a weekend picnic. Just be faithful to death: for ... *during those days a great number of you will be cast into prison and many will die ... just be faithful and you will live eternally with Me.*

*. I desire you to be certain that you understand that I do not want your works, and your using of My name, *when your beliefs entail those things which are corrupt and foreign to what I taught you to do.* I detest idolatry. *You know that.* I abhor fornication. *You know that.* Repent! Or you will perish and will not receive My wedding ring!

*. You need to 'know' that works, services and duties are not all that I require! Those who *'continue to indulge'* in their fornications and idolatries are against Me—and will go through that time of My Father's wrath: that dreaded *hour of testing which is coming to test all those who remain upon the earth.* It all depends upon what each one of your inward motives is. And I am definitely keeping a watch upon that. As I promised to all who would listen when I was on the earth, I will give rewards according to your works. I simply desire that you be sure that you are not trusting in some, or many, superficial works. If your works are truly done toward Me and you endure to the end you will reign with Me over all the nations; even as I have already promised to My chosen twelve apostles those thrones which are over the twelve tribes of Israel. And, you will rule then with a rod of iron!

*. Simply put, *I am interested in perfect works which are the natural outcome of your passion for Me. It is not what others think of your works that counts, but what I judge.* If you do not repent you will never know the time of My coming! Look around. There are many who truly love Me as their Lord, and their lives show it. *I promise you: love Me and you will live forever and I will personally introduce you as My Bride to My Father!*

*. Keep your faith in Me which believes that I am the One Who is able to open each and every door, and that no one is able to reverse My command. I want some of you to know that I realize that your works are 'righteous ones' done out of your true love for Me. And to you I renew My promise: I really will continue to open doors for you. In fact I will make the phoney church members serve you. They will see I love you and they will also know that I surely *pledge that the horrible time of My Father's wrath upon all mankind will NOT touch you.* Beloved, I will come quickly & I have your crown here waiting to be given to you. Truly I will complete My marriage vow to you!

*. Finally, in your doing your works, *do not be mediocre. Either serve Me passionately or forget Me altogether. But do not dilly dally around and claim that you are working for My Father and Me. I abhor that attitude.* You may think that you are rich; but I judge you to be wretched and miserable and poor and blind and naked. Still...I love you and urge you to obey Me without restraint. I will always be standing here at the door of your heart. I will always rap on your door. *Even as I will wait for the day you open to Me and ask Me to come and have true fellowship with you.* I truly request that you overcome evil, and, ultimately, that you reign with Me on the earth!"

John Enters Heaven

After those warnings and promises I looked up ... and saw into Heaven even as did Stephen our brother!

A door opened in Heaven!

An entrance through which one could enter into Jesus'other realm. A door through which I heard MY NAME called by the voice which in the very beginning of my vision sounded like a trumpet.

In the spirit I entered through that door.
Immediately I was in Heaven!

Immediately my attention was focused upon our Father's magnificent throne!What a sight! Especially looking upon Him Who sat on that rainbow-encircled throne!I was enthralled with how extremely grand everything was in His throneroom!

There were four resplendent, absolutely radiant, Heavenly creatures. They were surely the same which Ezekiel and other prophets had seen. I studied their wonderful form and heads for quite some time before I looked at twenty four elders who were seated around the throne.

Twenty four glorified human beings were seated around the throne. That sight of them simply melted me. Friends, now that I sit here writing this...I truly wonder if by our Lord's grace...if I might, in the future, be one of those elders I had seen up in Heaven worshipping Him. I do not know of course but for that matter I do not know why He chose me or any of the others to be one of the original 'twelve' in the first place.

---

*   *   *   *   *
The Little Scroll
*   *   *   *   *

I saw the One on the throne produce a little book in His hand. That scroll held my attention. *Instinctively, I knew that it was of the upmost importance!*

I stared at the scroll.

It was written both within and on its backside.

It was sealed with many seals: seven in all.

Soon, an angel came forth, and asked, "Who is worthy to open this scroll?" I did not know; *but I knew I did not feel worthy.* Nobody was worthy.

Nobody!

Nobody in Heaven. Nobody in the earth. Nobody under the earth. Not only could nobody open the seals off that scroll, there was not anyone found worthy to even look upon the words.

My emotions took over!

I wept.

I wept greatly.

I felt so depressed that I was not worthy enough. But I knew I was not. My eyelids could not contain the tears which flowed freely down my cheeks.

Years ago I had been Jesus' most beloved friend among the twelve, *but here in Heaven I was not worthy enough to do the angel's bidding.*

The tears continued to fall down my cheeks.

Certainly I felt worthless but I could not believe at first that there was not any, even of those twenty four who had been in Heaven for some time, who was worthy enough to look upon and open the little scroll. After much weeping...I was spoken to by one of those twenty four elders.

The elder, who apparently also was not worthy to do the task of opening the book, said, "Weep not, John. Behold! The LION of the tribe of Judah, the Root of David, has prevailed to open the book and to loose the seven seals thereof!"

The LION has Prevailed!

The LION of the tribe of Judah!

The Root, the Son, of David has prevailed!

The LION has prevailed in living a life in a manner that no other human has ever lived it! And, has been received back into Heaven as the **ONLY ONE WORTHY** to open and proclaim the words of God's Game Plan for the end of this grace-phase of man's existence upon this earth!

Not A Lion, A Lamb

However, into the midst of the Heavenly scene I saw not a LION *but a Lamb come*! A Lamb which looked as it had been slain. The Lamb advanced toward the throne. He took the scroll out of the right hand of the One who sat on the throne. Then He —THE LAMB!— allowed the four Heavenly creatures and the twenty four elders to fall down and sing a new song unto Him!

Even in the presence of the One on the throne!

The Lamb did not restrain the worshipful adoration which was being poured forth upon Him! The words of the song made it very clear to me Who this very precious Lamb was!

Oh, Lord Jesus!

I wept for joy as I heard the words: *"You are worthy to take the scroll & to open the seals for You were slain and You have redeemed us to God by Your blood. You have redeemed out of every kindred and tongue and people and nation those of us who You have made kings and priests unto our Lord God and we shall reign on the earth."*

The Lord's Day had just begun.

That is, the Day of the Lord.

The Day of the Lord had just begun and these redeemed ones were already anxiously accepting the time when they would be reigning upon the earth!

"We shall reign upon the earth."

(We should jump in here to present the following:

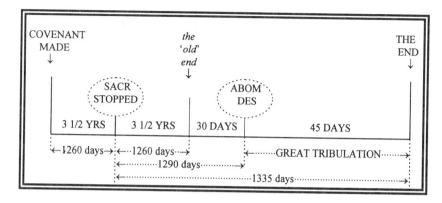

We are at the point of the Abomination of Desolation being placed or set up in the holy place. On our new 'wine skin' chart that comes 30 days after the end of Daniel's famous 70th week. The setting up takes place on the 1,290th day AFTER the stopping of the daily sacrifices in Jerusalem.

Jesus taught that at the time the Abomination of Desolation is set up that the Great Tribulation also begins.

On our chart the Great Tribulation begins then and lasts for forty-five days. Jesus' return to this Earth will end that horrible time of much suffering.)

EIGHT

Lucifer's Mistake

The Lord's Day has begun. It began because on the earth the **'abomination of desolation'** had been set up, and, once again, Lucifer discovered too late that what *he surmised would be his ultimate success over the Godhead was to become his defeat.*
His ultimate defeat.
Again.
Just like at the cross.
For again he gave the One on the throne the opportunity to present the ominous book of cursing and mournings and woe to His Son to break the seals and to read the words thereof.
If that evil one had only known, if he had only known, he would not have polluted the holy place with that most vile abomination which was THE ONE WICKED ACT which the Heavenly Father had long ago said would begin his judgment which would result again in ultimate desolation.
The one act which would bring forth the little book.
The one act which would allow the Lord to deal directly with His arch-enemy.
The one act which would begin the Lord's Day.
In Heaven all sensed that the Lamb's receiving of the little scroll was of the highest importance. It was not just the elders and the Heavenly creatures who sang with such pure praise and adoration! The Lamb's coming and His taking of the little book

out of the Father's right hand, brought forth a blast of Heavenly praise from ten thousand times ten thousands, and thousands of thousands, of angels singing forth with power and might:

Worthy!
Worthy!
Worthy!

Worthy is the Lamb that was slain
to receive POWER and RICHES and
WISDOM and STRENGTH and HONOUR
and GLORY and BLESSING!

It did not stop there!
Oh, Lord Jesus!
Soon creatures in Heaven, on earth, under the earth, and in the seas were praising both the Father and the Lamb!

BLESSING and HONOUR
and GLORY and POWER be
unto Him that sits upon the throne
and unto the Lamb for ever and ever!
For ever and ever!

The singing and adulation went on and on.
To both the Father and the Lamb.
It went on and on.
On and on.
On and on.

The Unsealing Of The Scroll

When the singing finally ended it brought forth the time of the unsealing of the scroll and of the reading of its contents—of its mysterious contents. *The Father's book of utter judgment and woe for the end of this day of grace lay sealed in the hands of the Lamb.*

Ezekiel had a vision almost identical to mine. That man of God also saw the heavens open. Instead of going upward as I was instructed to do, however, God came down to his world!

Our Lord came riding down upon the same opulent throne which I saw in Heaven: for that throne is carried to and fro wherever He wants to go.

Ezekiel has seen the same four Heavenly creatures I saw. As with other old testament writers, he also saw some wheels upon which the flying throne moved. With both of our visions, and as Isaiah also saw, the Lord God came in a processional coronation which would have topped any celebration given by the heraldry of our world!

Ezekiel looked to the north and saw a great cloud and a fire infolding itself. There was a huge brightness surrounding it all. Out of the *'midst of the brilliant fire'* there was a form which appeared as the color of amber. As it came closer to him he saw a platform as of a magnificent crystal. Above that platform, he saw the throne as the appearance of a sapphire stone and on the throne he saw what appeared to him to be the likeness of a man. Indeed, from that fiery form on the throne the brilliant glory of the Lord emanated!

It was so like what I saw!

When Ezekiel actually saw His brilliance, he fell upon his face as dead: even as I did recently. When a voice told him to stand upon his feet, the spirit likewise entered into him and he stood: even as happened to me recently.

"Son of man," the voice said to him after he had risen from the ground, "I send you to the children of Israel...a nation...has rebelled against Me...even unto this very day...whether they will hear or whether they will forbear, yet shall they know that there has been a prophet among them. But, hear what I say to you. Be not rebellious like that rebellious house. Open your mouth, and eat what I give you."

Oh, I weep with so strong emotion
even as I rehearse these words. His experience was
so like unto mine own.

When Ezekiel looked, behold, a hand held out a scroll to him. The hand spread the roll out before him, and he saw that it was written WITHIN and on the BACKSIDE. Just like the one I saw in Heaven. His was not sealed, he noticed that it was full of lamentations and mournings and woe.

He obeyed and ate the scroll.

It filled his belly.

But catch this...when it was in his mouth it was as sweet as honey! However, when it entered his belly he soon went forth in bitterness, in the heat of his spirit.

The scroll was sweet to his mouth but was bitter within his belly. Soon in my book I will share how I too was given the scroll that was in Jesus' hand and was told to eat it."Take it and eat it up. It shall be in your mouth sweet as honey, but, it shall make your belly bitter," He told me!

The little scroll Ezekiel ate dealt with the final 'absolute' destruction of Jerusalem back in his day. That scroll he ate was the *'type'* of the one which I saw in Heaven in our Lord God's right hand.

Our Lord presents vivid pictures or 'types' all through His dealings with us humans so that we can easily understand what He desires to share with us. Ezekiel's scroll is a great example of such pictures.

In each case a Heavenly personage has the roll. In each case a committed follower of the Lord is commanded to eat it, and, in each case, the scroll is sweet in the mouth and bitter in the belly. And, as I have sensed, the one in the Lamb's hand as the Day of the Lord begins is one that is also full of horrifying lamentations and mournings and woe.

The Unsealing Begins

I felt I needed to share that with you as I now tell of the unsealing of the book. Jesus began breaking the seals and with each seal that He broke off there was a corresponding judgment or event upon the earth. The Lord's Day had begun, therefore, each of these judgments on the earth occur under the authority and control and will of the Lord, and of His angels, and of the Heavenly Control Center.

A similar set of events to those I saw in the first four seals took place back in Zechariah's day in the Old Covenant time. In his vision, he saw four chariots coming into view: in the first set were red horses, in the second black horses, in the third he saw white horses, and in the fourth dappled and bay horses.

"What are these?" he asked.

The answer was that the horses *were the four spirits of the heavens that go forth from standing before the Lord of all the earth*. In the matter of the black and the white horses which he had seen, they traveled into the north country ... and Zechariah was *informed that they 'quieted the Lord's spirit' in the north country*.

As back in Zechariah's time, all the horses sent forth in my vision are *from the bidding of the Lord*. It is God's Game Plan and the breaking of each of the seals results in an act directed from His throne.

In the breaking of the first seal, there was a sending forth of a white horse & his rider who went conquering and to conquer. (Possibly they also went into the north country, into the same territory as in Zechariah's day).

In the breaking of the second seal...a red horse and rider were sent from Heaven to take peace from the earth. *First, they go conquering and to conquer. Second, there is the removal of peace from the earth.*

The two combine for a successful mission.

At the breaking of the third seal, a black horse and rider came before the throne with a pair of scales. That scene is *one of famine or one of plenty*. (In a similar story back in Elisha's day, that prophet promises that the measure of fine flour will be sold the next day for a shekel, and two measures of barley for a shekel. Back in that narrative we have the grand advantage of a contemporary saying, "Behold, might this thing be if the Lord would make windows in heaven."

We therefore have a statement which allows us to 'see' that Elisha meant that on the morrow there would be *aplenty*. In the Revelation the voice speaks forth, "A measure of wheat for a penny, and three measures of barely for a penny." Is it feast, or is it famine? Oh,to have a contemporary fellow pipe up and say it meant famine or plenty. *It could be famine, but whichever it is, it will be sorely bad or abounding plenty.)*

The breaking of the fourth seal authorized a pale horse with a rider named Death and Hades. Power was given to them over the fourth of the earth to kill with the sword, with hunger, with death, and with the beasts of the earth.

The first four seal judgments come from the Control Center in Heaven. From the 'dictates' of our Lord Almighty. All those judgments have been promised throughout the entire scriptures. Similar such judgments have taken place throughout the eras of our earth's existence. These are harsh times, nevertheless, *the much harsher time of the pouring out of God's wrath has not yet come.*

Believers Massacred

This seal is the time that Jesus instructed would come at the end of this age of grace He began with the first four seals:

> "You shall hear of wars and rumours of wars. See that you be not troubled, for all these things must come to pass.
>
> "But the end is not yet. For nation shall rise against nation and kingdom against kingdom, and there shall be famines..pestilences..earthquakes in a multitude of places. All these are the beginning of sorrows."

He then continued with the fifth and sixth seals:

> "Then shall they deliver you up to be afflicted and shall kill you and you shall be hated of all nations for My name sake...many shall be offended & shall betray one another & shall hate one another."

In my vision, the breaking of the next seal brought the same troubling time period for believers worldwide. When our Jesus opened the fifth seal, I saw under the altar in Heaven the *souls* of them that *were 'murdered' for the word of God and for the testimony which they held!*

This seal was against Christians...but even it was under the guiding control of our loving Heavenly Father. Jesus told me to write to one of the faithful churches (the one named Smyrna) that they would have tribulation for ten days, & because of its harshness that they should be faithful unto death.

I watched and listened to the *martyred bodyless souls who had been faithful unto death* and I realized that praying for our God to avenge them was the pleading concern for the moment: "How long ... do You not judge, and avenge our blood on them that dwell on the earth?" These souls were given white robes to wear. These souls had form.

They were then told that they should WAIT yet for a *'short season'* until *others of their fellow servants and their brethren should be killed.*

A Mistaken Assumption

The breaking of the sixth seal shows that our Lord God was not pleased with the death of so many of His children. It was so harsh (ie, the sixth seal) it brought forth by all the wicked upon the earth this mistaken cry, "Doomsday! Doomsday!"

Let me repeat:

The sixth seal was so harsh it brought forth the mistaken cry from the wicked on the earth. "Doomsday!" <u>The time of wrath HAD NOT YET COME, but the wicked on the earth thought it had,</u> and yelled:

"<u>Doomsday!</u>

In that seal breaking, there was a great earthquake, the sun became black, the moon red, and stars fell **(not the stars 'out there':** the thousands and tens of thousands of space satellites and space junk we have been inundating our upper atmosphere with for the last few decades. Seen 'burning' in our atmosphere as they fall earthbound at very high speeds, they were viewed by

John as falling 'stars').

The breaking of the sixth seal IS the most fearful time up to that point in the Lord's Day, nevertheless, *take note of who is doing all the shouting & who is claiming that the time of His wrath is come.*

Neither the Lord, nor His Son, nor His angels claim that the "time of His wrath is come." They do not claim any such thing. Only wicked men mistakenly do.

It is only scared-to-death wicked rulers who wrongfully claim that is the time of His wrath. The kings of the earth and the great men, and the chief captains and the mighty men and every slave and every freeman hid in the dens and in the rocks of the mountain, and said (so foolishly) to the mountains and rocks, "Fall on us and hide us from the face of Him that sits on the throne, and from the wrath of the Lamb. For the great day of His wrath is come, and who is able to stand it?"

> *Who is crying, "Doomsday has come!"*
> *Who thinks that, "Doomsday has come!"*
> *Who is crying, "The great day of His wrath is come!"*
> *Who thinks that, "The great day of His wrath is come!"*
> *Only wicked men mistakenly do.*

Friends, every word they cry is wrong.

It is wrong.

Not Wrath, Calmness

For I did not see wrath being poured out next. Instead I saw just the **opposite**. I saw four angels holding the four winds of the earth that the winds should not blow on the earth nor on the sea, nor on any tree.

It was peace and calm.

Not the time of the wrath of God.

As the breaking of that same seal continued the angels were told to not hurt anything til the servants of God from Israel were sealed. Friends, instead of the wrath of God being poured out in the sixth seal **per** the wicked men, I saw the gracious sealing for protection of an hundred and forty four thousand men of Israel!

No, wicked leaders of this earth, neither doomsday—nor God's
wrath—comes in the breaking of the sixth seal.

Many of our brethren might have wished that it HAD drawn
down our Lord's wrath against the wicked of the earth because,
during that lull and during the sealing of those 144,000 faithful
Israelites another multitude of thousands of suffering Christians
were slain. For I beheld a host which 'no man could number' of
all nations and kindred and people and tongues standing *before*
the throne and before the Lamb clothed in white robes & with
palms in their hands.

One of the twenty four elders asked me:

"Who are these which are arrayed in
white robes and from where did they come?"

I replied to him,
"You know. I certainly do not."

The elder answered,
"These are they which have
come out of great tribulation
and have washed their robes
and made them white in
the blood of the Lamb."

These are the brethren those souls of the fifth seal were told
would also be martyred for their faithful Christian stand. Those
first martyrs were told to wait a short season for the rest of their
brethren who would be coming home.

These are the rest of them.

Now HOME together they are before the throne of God and
together they serve Him day and night.

They shall hunger no more as they did in their suffering in
those first days of the great tribulation.

They shall thirst no more as they did in the suffering during
those first days of the great tribulation.

Neither shall the sun light on them, nor any heat.

For the Lamb which is in the midst of the throne shall feed them and He shall lead them unto living fountains of waters, & God shall wipe away all tears from their eyes.

Finally the sixth seal events came to an end.

The Book Is Ready To Be Read

Jesus then broke the last seal to be broken before the scroll could be read. That of course **IS THE REASON** for the breaking of the seals by the Lamb. There is no 'mystic-symbol meaning' to be given to the breaking of the seven seals. They NEEDED TO BE BROKEN TO ENABLE the unrolling of the scroll by Jesus so that He could read it!

Why accept the little book out of the hand of Him Who sat on the throne if He was not intending to read the little book? (Again, those seven seals, and the seven trumpets and the seven vials are not three sets of seven mystical objects hanging somewhere in this story which we students of scripture are at liberty to place anywhere we want in the end time scenario. Revelation is a continuing story & vision which John saw & lived through and that happened in a chronological order. Friends, there is no telescoping even hinted at in his rendering of his vision.

The sole purpose of the breaking of the seven seals by Jesus is so that He can get to the much more important job of reading the words of the little scroll.

Let me repeat that:

The sole purpose of the breaking of the seven seals by Jesus is so that He can get to the much more important job of reading the words of the little scroll.

That sole purpose was made emphatic by the fact that at the breaking of the seventh seal he saw no event or judgment take place on the earth. No event corresponded to the breaking of the final seal of that little scroll.

There needed to be no such event...for John saw Jesus open the totally unsealed book.

The ominous book of woe was ready to be read.)

Half Hour Of Silence

In Heaven we stood waiting in total silence for half an hour. Silence. Complete silence. Overwhelming silence. Never did any of the creatures, nor any of the elders, nor of the angels, nor any other being make a sound for a half hour.

All we did was wait.

We knew our place.

We also were **ready to hear Jesus begin** with His reading of the mysterious little book.

None of us talked.

Or sang.

Or wept.

And of course there was no outpouring of the wrath of God. That was to come soon enough. But AFTER the breaking of the seventh seal the important essence was that the scroll was open and all in attendance in Heaven were waiting for the words of the little book to flow out of Jesus' mouth!

One half hour of muted silence we waited.

He in turn was WAITING for the signal from His Father to begin with the reading.

We all saw His readiness to trust the Father in that.

Thus we also were willing to trust the Father for that.

We would have waited hours, days, and weeks if that were called for. However, it was not.

Only one half hour.

To my surprise, Jesus was not told to begin reading. Instead I saw seven 'called' angels assemble before the throne.

To each angel was given a golden trumpet.

Why? It became obvious: *the golden trumpets were to be an official fanfare to announce the reading of God's written scroll.*

---

(1) I first saw the seals ripped off the little scroll so it could be read.

(2) I then saw the seven golden trumpets sound forth to announce the reading of the little book.

(3) I finally saw the reading of the book begin. At the same time the pouring out of the wrath of God began: for the little book was exactly the completeness of that. It was the words which were full of lamentations, mournings, and woes.

(It is a very chronological story from beginning to end. First, John sees Jesus is here on the earth as the Mighty One to protect His church as the Day of the Lord, the Lord's Day, begins. He is then taken to the Heavenly Control Center. He sees the little book presented. Jesus is the only One worthy enough to open it so He takes the book and begins breaking the seals off. At the point that it is ready to be read, Jesus with the scroll open waits with all as the Father calls seven angels forward.

Each angel is given a golden trumpet to sound to announce the solemn reading of the book. Thus there was to be no reading of the scroll's contents until those seven angels sound forth with their trumpets.

It's a simple storyline to follow, isn't it. Why have 'theologians' so garbled it up? Why? Primarily because the Lord sealed a major piece of the puzzle so none could know what He was planning to do until the 'time of the end.')

The Seven Trumpets

I saw an angel come forth with a golden censer. To him was given much incense to be offered with the prayers of all saints–including the avenging prayers of those slain saints in Heaven (those who died and went to Heaven in the fifth and sixth seals) as well as all the urgent bequests of the Christians STILL down upon the earth. The smoky mixture ascended up before God.

He smelled it. He heard it.

However, there was other work to be done first.

The angel took the censer, filled it with fire from the altar in Heaven and cast it into the earth. I thought as I saw that violent display of power, **if that is any sign,** and I was sure it was, the sounding of the that set of trumpets was going to be a lot more tumultuous than was the breaking of the seals.

I was astonished with what followed.

The first angel sounded his trumpet and the third part of the trees and the green grass burned up!

The second sounded & the third part of the creatures in the sea died and the third part of the ships were quickly destroyed!

The third sounded & the third of rivers and of the fountains of waters became bitter, causing many to die!

The fourth sounded and the third part of the sun and of the moon and of the stars was smitten so that a third part of the day and night did not shine!

Quickly four angels had sounded.

There were three trumpets left.

Another angel flew through the air, crying:

> **"WOE!**
>
> **"WOE!**
>
> **"WOE!"**

The three woes were directed toward the 'inhabitants of the earth by reason of the three trumpets which are yet to sound!'

The First Woe

The fifth trumpet sounded.

The bottomless pit was opened!

Smoke arose out of it and out of the smoke came beings that were commanded to hurt only those men which had not the seal of their God in their foreheads. It was that they should not kill them, but that the men should be tormented five months: 'those men' would seek death in those days and shall not find it; they shall desire death, and it shall flee from them. That judgment was the first woe to come upon those who were lacking God's seal.

(These demons, these captive fallen angels, were allowed to indulge themselves by inflicting loathsome pain on those living on the earth with the *only exception* being those with God's *seal* upon them.

In our new wine skin chart those five months would ride at least three months into the millennium.

Can that be? Decidedly so. I see this inflictment of terrifying pain as the main reason that those sheep and goats nations will be brought to our Lord Jesus Christ. Those nation will hear that 'healing' can once again be had in Jerusalem.

The nations will come to the promise land for their healing. And at that time they will be separated into either sheep or goat nations.)

The Second Woe

The sixth trumpet sounded.

Four angels were loosed from the river Euphrates. These four were prepared for precisely that moment in time to slay a third part of men. Under them was an army of 200,000,000— two hundred thousand thousand. Sadly, the rest of the men who were not killed by these plagues *did not repent* of the works of their hands. They continued to worship devils and idols of gold and silver and brass and stone and of wood...statues which can see nor hear nor walk.

Neither repented they of their murders.

Nor of their sorceries.

Nor of their fornications.

Nor of their thefts.

The Mighty Messenger

STILL IN THE SIXTH TRUMPET and IN THE SECOND WOE, I saw a mighty Messenger come down from Heaven.

He was clothed with a cloud.

A rainbow was upon His head.

His face was as it were the sun. His feet as pillars of fire.

I knew it was our Lord Jesus Christ. To confirm that certain belief, the mighty One coming to the earth *had the little book in His hand.* Since He had already broken off all the seals, the book of course *was 'open' in His hand.*

Jesus set his right foot upon the sea and His left foot on the earth. We were back in our land. He shouted with a loud voice. That shouting was followed with seven thunders uttering their voices. I started to write down what they said but was hindered from doing so.

(Those utterings will be very significant in the coming Day of the Lord. During the sixth trumpet, all will hear the words of the thunders' utterings. All nations, languages and tongues will clearly hear those ominous pleadings. *Since the timing is just before the sounding of the all important last seventh trumpet those seven utterances will have grave significance.* Great and wonderful significance! No wonder their words were sealed for the present!

When the thunders finish I believe there will not be any on this earth who will not know that the LAST trumpet is about to sound. Our Lord does not want any to perish...still, way too many will not heed to these utterances either.

Like we noticed back at the beginning of this study, our Creator of all has added in a number of ingenious novelties to make the study of End Time prophecy overwhelming. Here is 'another' one such novelty. The sealing of these seven thunders.

Their words, if they had been recorded down,
would have apparently added immediate understanding
to this portion of His Game Plan.

But NO He said.
And the words were sealed.)

There Shall Be Time No Longer

Standing upon the sea and the earth, Jesus lifted His hand toward Heaven and swore, "There shall be time no longer."

> *It was instantly clear to me.*
> *There would be no more time to enter His Body, to enter that group that He was going to take home at the sounding of the last trumpet.*

There was time no longer to be saved.
There was time no longer to become a true follower of His.
The DAY of grace was ceasing.
The first ten days of tribulation were nearly up.
He made this extremely plain in His next statement:

"In the days of the voice of the seventh angel,
when he shall begin to sound, the mystery of God
should be finished."

As soon as the seventh (last) angel sounds his trumpet, at the very instant he begins to blow, the 'mystery of God' would be ended finished...completed. The gathering together of Jews and Gentiles into His body would be complete!
What an awesome promise!
May I repeat that:
As soon as the 'last' angel sounds his trumpet, **at the very instant he begins to blow**, the mystery of God would be ended, finished...completed. The gathering together of Jews & Gentiles into His body would be complete!
And He gave it to me!
Oh, thank You, my Lord!

The Mystery Of God

Concerning the 'mystery', Jesus used the term three times—once in the singular and twice in the plural but it always meant the same thing. In the parable of the sower He stated, Unto you it is given to know the 'mystery' of the kingdom of God. In the parable Jesus taught how believers would fill up the kingdom of God here on the earth: the Word would be sown and people would receive it in various ways, and, only those who heard it, and received that word in good ground would, in turn, sow it, and thereby bring forth fruit, some thirtyfold, some sixty, and some an hundred.

The mystery of the kingdom of God which Jesus began was the 'formation and growth of the church:' the body of Christ. The mystery of the kingdom was therefore equal to the building of the church.

Referring to this same mystery, Paul wrote to the Romans that the reason for the present blindness of Israel is for the great purpose *OF BRINGING IN* the fullness of the Gentiles into the kingdom of God. He added that it was a mystery for it was kept secret from since the world began.

Gentiles Fellow-heirs With Jews

To those in Ephesus, Paul wrote, "You may understand my knowledge in the 'mystery' of Christ, *which in other ages was not made known unto the sons of men,* as it is now revealed unto His holy apostles and prophets by the Spirit; *THAT THE GENTILES SHOULD BE FELLOW-HEIRS, and of the same body, and partakers of His promise in Christ by the gospel."*

(With all that in mind when John was taken in the spirit to Heaven and was instructed to write Revelation, he was shown the rapture. I do not mean he was shown some *'SYMBOLIC'* hocus-pocus like his own command to 'Come up hither'. *John was shown the actual rapture taking place with Jesus doing the wonderful task of harvesting us Home!* What John was granted in that vision AGREED in every aspect to what Jesus,

Paul, Peter and the rest were shown concerning that wondrous 'glorious' coming day for all true believers in our Christ Jesus. And as we would now expect having read this so far, the rapture takes place *IN the Great Tribulation and AT the last trumpet.*

Here's our chart with this added knowledge:

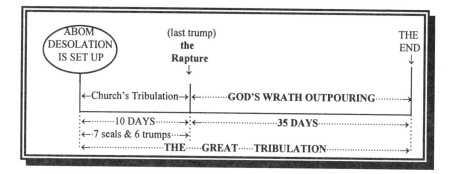

Thus, we find that the seven seal-breakings and the first six trumpet soundings come in those initial ten DAYS of the Great Tribulation.

That's a lot to happen, but can you imagine how much rain poured forth, and how much disrupture of the earth's skin burst across our planet, and how many 'fountains of the deep' gushed and spumed, in the initial ten days of the Flood?

A horribly enormous total had to have swamped our globe for it to be totally submerged by the end of forty days.

And deluged it was.

The Rapture: The Last Trumpet

We shall not all sleep (die), but we shall all be changed. In a moment, in the twinkling of an eye, at the last trump(et). For the trumpet shall sound and the dead shall be raised incorruptible and those still alive shall be changed.

Jesus said, When the angel BEGINS to sound, the mystery of God should be completed! The very nanosecond it begins to sound the *formation of the Body of Christ* from both Jews and Gentiles would be accomplished! *As the last trumpet* **begins to sound** *the completion of the formation of His Body will have taken place.*

Concerning the Rapture, Paul wrote that it would take place (1) in a moment, (2) in the twinkling of an eye, (3) & at the last trumpet. He told us that it would occur when our Lord descends from Heaven with a shout, with the voice of the archangel, and with the trumpet of God...and that the 'raptured ones' would be caught up together in the clouds to meet Him in the air.

Concerning that *'day and hour'*, Jesus said that no man, no angel, nor He Himself knew when it would occur: that only His Father knew the exact moment of the rapture.

Let me repeat the words of Jesus:

> *"In the days of the voice of the seventh angel, when he shall begin to sound, the mystery of God should be finished."*

Sounds like that 'in-a-moment, in-the-twinkling-of-an-eye, last-trumpet' rapture of the church to me, friends.

I hope you cannot wait to 'see and hear' what happens the very moment, the very instant, that seventh trumpet begins to sound!

Eat The Scroll, John

It was at that moment that He gave me the little scroll, and told me to take it and to eat it. I obeyed and it was in my mouth sweet as honey, but when it got down into my belly: it was very bitter.

I was then given a REED to measure the temple of God and the altar and them that worship therein. I was to measure only that. I was not to measure the 'outer court' of the Gentiles. For at that point in the coming Lord's Day it would still be given unto the Gentiles.

Of course, there was also no actual TEMPLE building there.

I was like the man in Zechariah's vision who was also given a measuring line to measure Jerusalem when it lay desolated in ruin. We both were surveying the land for future projects. (See Zech. 2:1-5, & 1:12-16.) Mine, of course, was to prepare the way for Jesus' rebuilding of the third Temple Himself ... even as it has been prophesied of Him by Zechariah..

This is all happening in that sixth trumpet & in that second woe.

For the last (seventh) trumpet is yet to be sounded.

Still In The Sixth Trumpet

Next ... I saw two witnesses who had been prophesying for three and a half years in their capital wearing sackcloth. During their years of preaching nobody could harm them.

They were invincible.

However, when they finished their testimony they no longer had the Lord's protection; and, at the appointed time, they were overcome and killed and laid in the streets of Jerusalem for the purpose of being looked upon and of being mocked by all who passed by.

At that point in the Lord's Day ... those that dwelt upon the earth rejoiced over their deaths, and made merry, and sent gifts one to another because the two murdered 'outspoken' prophets had tormented them greatly.

After the pair had lain there three and a half days, and, as I watched, our Lord God's 'Spirit of life' entered into them, and they stood up on their feet, and I felt the enormous fear which fell upon all that saw them!

The two then heard a great voice from Heaven calling them to: Come up hither! They heard it, I heard it also and all around the people heard it! The two ascended up to Heaven in a cloud while their enemies beheld them.

(*Tom here again:* I hope we see that it is only the slaying of those two prophets and their coming back to life after three and a half days, and their ascending to Heaven which FITS into the timing here in the closing moments of the sixth trumpet. Do not attempt to place their entire three & a half year ministry in this particular scene. The two had been ministering in Jerusalem for that long—and that is important!--but John only wants us to see that at this point in the sixth trumpet they were killed and that they lay in the street for a few days and then were taken up into Heaven by the Spirit.)

The same hour there was a great earthquake causing a tenth part of Jerusalem to fall! It was a devastating earthquake which killed seven thousand men: the remnant in the city were scared and gave glory to God!

That ended the sixth trumpet and the second woe.

That was a long trumpet happening.

The third woe comes quickly.

TEN

New Set Of Great Voices In Heaven

The seventh angel sounded.
AND THERE WERE GREAT VOICES IN HEAVEN!
Rivers of voices before and all around the throne!

Great voices which were not there seconds earlier!

Friends, there was such a change in Heaven! One second, *no humongus crowd up there around the throne; the next, WHAT A CROWD!*

What an innumerable crowd of glorified worshippers!

Absolutely mind-boggling!

It was astounding to me to hear, to see, the entire 'raptured church' singing! As were the words of the new song they were singing:

"THE KINGDOMS OF THIS WORLD ARE BECOME THE KINGDOMS OF OUR LORD AND OF HIS CHRIST, AND HE SHALL REIGN FOR EVER AND EVER!"

Surely you are catching the glory of it!

I had been intently watching the whole scene leading up to the sounding of that last trumpet and when that angel began to sound, when he BEGAN to sound forth...I HEARD A BRAND NEW HUGE CHOIR SINGING FORTH IN HEAVEN!

I heard and saw the risen church of Jesus Christ!

Let me repeat:

> *I had been intently watching the whole scene leading up to the sounding of that seventh trumpet, and when that angel began to sound, when he BEGAN to sound forth...I HEARD A *BRAND *NEW *HUGE *CHOIR SINGING FORTH IN HEAVEN!*

I heard a whole NEW set of singers bellowing out as NEW great voices in Heaven. I do not have space to describe the new voices here. But very, very soon, I will describe them.

What I have to tell you about that loudly-singing group will **simply thrill you!** Friends, those of you who are LIVING when the seventh trumpet begins to sound will be caught up from the earth and will then be, *as one body with its Head*, ushered up to the Lord's throne with your own Husband, Jesus Christ! All the dead in Christ up to that time will of course also be rising with you at that exalted moment!

For now just let me tell you that God's Game Plan has been set up since the foundation of the world so that coming Home-coming of His Son's Bride would be the CENTRAL aim of the very beginning moments of the reading of that woe-filled book Jesus had opened and was ready to read.

> *Immediately I knew that Home-coming*
> *was the sweetness both Ezekiel and I tasted*
> *when we ate that little scroll.*

At that moment there had been no cataclysmic 'happening' down on earth even though another trumpet had just sounded.

That *bitterness* would soon take over.

But first the sweetness.

The new group of singing raptured believers in Heaven, and the twenty four elders falling on their faces to worship the ONE on the throne with these praise-filled words of high gratitude:

We give You thanks, O Lord God Almighty,
BECAUSE YOU HAVE TAKEN TO YOU YOUR GREAT
POWER AND HAVE REIGNED! The nations were angry
and Your wrath IS come (the righteous men finally are
claiming that God's wrath IS come.)
AND THE TIME OF THE DEAD
THAT THEY SHOULD BE JUDGED,
AND THAT YOU SHALL GIVE REWARDS
TO YOUR SERVANTS THE PROPHETS, AND TO THE
SAINTS AND TO THEM THAT FEAR YOUR NAME,
SMALL AND GREAT.

The time has also come that You should
destroy them which destroy the earth.

(We will pass over chapters twelve and thirteen for the time being because chronologically they DO NOT fit in here. They, like the section which said the two witnesses had ministered for three and a half years, have been correctly placed there by John as background chapters to show how this world became so vile that our loving Heavenly Father was now JUST to pour out His pure, unadulterated wrath.

In a future book, I will come back to visit these background chapters for they certainly are so very important to our study of the End Times. But for now, we will skip over them and move to chapter fourteen where John continues his moving prophetic vision of the End Times.

Let me repeat.

John realized what he was doing when he placed chapters twelve and thirteen where he placed them. They are needed as background material to understand the JUSTNESS of what is to follow. However, they do not fit in chronologically here.

Chapter fourteen chronologically follows the end verses of chapter eleven.)

Revelation 14

At the beginning of the sounding of that seventh trumpet I heard the new group of great voices in Heaven singing unto our great God and unto His Son Jesus Christ.

Of course I now continue at that same scene: right back with that new group in Heaven. And with the righteous 144,000 now in Jerusalem! That remnant of the city which believed would so need God's protection since the pouring out of the wrath was to very soon commence.

Friends, I SAW Jesus, as the Lamb of God, standing in the midst of those 144,000 men. Even as I had seen our Lord Jesus standing in the midst of the churches as the Lord's DAY began, now they have just been taken Home, and He is standing in the midst of the 144,000 to be THEIR protection since the harshest portion of the Great Tribulation is to begin. This protection of Jesus standing in the midst of those faithful Jewish men and of their families is one more aspect of the wonderful sweetness at the first eating of the little scroll.

As the last angel began to sound, the spiritual offspring of Abraham will be protected from the outpouring of the wrath to come by being raptured Home. Thus, I saw the raptured church in Heaven.

I also saw Jesus, as the Lamb of God, standing in the midst of the 144,000 natural children of Abraham, <u>even as I saw Him willingly stand in the midst of the churches at the beginning of the Lord's Day to be with the Christians during their ten days of great tribulation. He stood with them as the **'Mighty One.'**</u> <u>Now</u>, with His Bride safely home in Heaven, <u>He stands in the midst of the true and faithful Israelis, not as the Mighty One, but as their **'Lamb'**, as their Passover Lamb, as their Redeemer, as the One for Whom they are still looking.</u>

---

     *   *   *   *   *   *   *

And they instantly become 'partakers' of those who believe in the Lamb as their Messiah and coming King.Even as brother Paul had prophesied. Their blindness would disappear when the fullness of the Gentiles had come in.

The fullness of the Gentiles just went to Heaven with Jesus in the rapture and these 144,000 men lose their blindness at that same moment!

     *   *   *   *   *   *   *

At that same moment, friends!

Just as he prophesied.

The 144,000 will go through the outpouring of the wrath of God here upon the earth, and, certainly they have MISSED the Rapture, but they will have Jesus their Messiah right there with them in their presence during that harsh time of Jacob's trouble. He will be with the men even as He stood back in their history with Shadrach, Meshach and Abednego within the hot burning fiery furnace which had been heated seven times hotter than it was wont to be heated!

And those three, with Him, had no hurt!

Upon whose bodies the fire had no power, nor was an hair of their head singed, neither were their coats changed, nor had the smell of fire passed on them. (Dan.3:27.)

Friends, the only safe place on the earth during the coming 'fire and brimstone' rain of wrath will be where Christ resides! Especially where He resides as the Passover Lamb of God! All who gather with Him will be untouched by the raging torrents of plagues: even as those who trusted wholeheartedly in the blood of the Passover lambs in the land of Egypt were left with neither a scar nor a death in their homes in the land of Goshen.

Thus, my first thought is to tell of the very safe haven Jesus has prepared for the faithful sealed 144,000. No wonder the eating of that little scroll was so very very sweet to my mouth! In the first instance *the church has left this old world for Glory* ... and in the second, *Jesus is standing right in the midst of His chosen men down on earth.*

Now back to the raptured great voices in Heaven!

The voices I heard were as the voice of many waters, and as the voice of a great thunder, and as the voice of harpers harping with their harps. It was overwhelming as well as very beautiful. And they sang a new song before the throne. It was a song that no one except the 144,000 on earth could sing. My mentioning the 144,000 does not mean that all of the next descriptions refer to them. It will be clear that with the various descriptions I refer not to them but to the raptured Christians in Heaven.

The Raptured Church Described

*Those who made up the great voice in Heaven were those who were redeemed FROM THE EARTH–they were finally in Heaven. A goal to which all believers look forward.

*They were not defiled with women.

*They followed the Lamb withersoever He went (of course, only Christians can testify to being followers of Jesus most, or all, of their lives. Certainly the faithful 144,000 Jews could not have claimed to be followers of Jesus up until the very moment when for the first time in their lives He stands in their midst as their Passover Lamb. It's too bad, but prior to His coming into their midst, they had continually rejected His claim as being the One they should accept as their Messiah).

*They were redeemed FROM AMONG MEN (the faithful 144,000 were still here on the earth among men). But those in Heaven had finally crossed that long bridge and were Home at last.

*They were the firstfruits unto God and to the Lamb! Thus, the harvest they were a part of was the smaller 'firstfruits' one. The 'first resurrection' does not take place until near the end of this book I am writing on the Revelation. And the much larger angelic harvesting of the *good seed* will also come later. It will be done after Jesus returns at the end of this age.

I purposely use this term to describe the raptured Christians in Heaven. As Jesus was the 'firstfruits from the dead', so these raptured ones are the 'firstfruits' of all who believe in Him, and of all who will be resurrected from the earth.

The 'later' first resurrection will be a wonderful event in which to take part. Yet, each and everyone in that innumerable throng of 'post-Rapture' believers HAVE TO DIE in the Great Tribulation. Many of those who rose in the Rapture never died. But ALL who partake in the first resurrection will have died the death of a martyr.

Those who are brought back to life in that resurrection are re-united with their bodies *'after'* He comes back to earth to reign. And *'after'* Jesus has Satan 'bound and cast' into the bottomless pit for the entire Lord's Day, for the entire thousand years, they will also REIGN with Christ during the entire Lord's Day. That will be the first resurrection.

These singing up in Heaven at the beginning of the seventh trumpet are not involved with the much larger angelic harvesting at the end of the age NOR with the 'first resurrection.' I therefore make use of the term 'FIRSTFRUITS' because any fruit that is thus called, is, by its very name, picked BEFORE the FINAL HARVEST of the fruit (the good seed) at the end of the growing season!

The redeemed believers singing the new song in Heaven are, of course, precisely that! They are firstfruits unto God and unto the Lamb. In any farming culture, the 'firstfruits' always have a special place and taste in the peoples' minds.

More Descriptions Of The Raptured Church

Hold on, there is more!

I was told much about the great new multitude in Heaven!

*In their mouth was found no guile, for they are WITHOUT FAULT BEFORE THE THRONE OF GOD! Before the throne in Heaven they are found with no guile! And without fault!

I believe that is astounding!

I was so overflowing with joy as I watched those believers gathered before the throne without fault!

I give our Lord Jesus all the credit for that wonderful truth! Brother Paul also gives our Lord Jesus Christ all the credit:

> *"Who shall also confirm you unto the end*
> *that ye may be blameless*
> *in the day of our Lord Jesus Christ." (I Cor.1:8)*

That resplendent fact is exactly what I saw about those who were singing before the throne. They were blameless. **Praise God,** they were blameless! Look at all this:

> ** *I saw the raptured church sing a new song in Heaven as the last trumpet began to sound. It was even as Jesus had declared to me:*
> ** *In the days of the voice of the seventh angel, when he shall begin to sound, the mystery of God will be finished. At that instant!*
> ** *They were redeemed FROM the earth.*
> ** *They were not defiled with women.*
> ** *They were followers of the Lamb wheresoever*

> *He led.*
> ** *They were redeemed FROM among men.*
> ** *They were the firstfruits unto God, and to the*
> *Lamb.*
> ** *They were with NO GUILE in their mouths.*
> ** *They were without fault BEFORE the throne*
> *of God in Heaven.*

(What a set of descriptions! One will not find a 'more clear and complete picture' of the raptured Christians standing with no guile and without fault before the throne of God and singing before Him in Heaven anywhere else in the scriptures.

I plead with you.

Accept Him today–and follow Him withersoever He leads. For this firstfruits Rapture is the *raising upward* that you truly want to be involved in.

Those who make it to the 'first resurrection' will be blessed –truly blessed–but look at all the 'added torture' they will have to go through before, and up to, their martyrdom.

I plead with you.

Follow Jesus, today.

We Promised This

Remember our word to you:

The truth is that even as it should the book of Revelation does give to all who study its pages the clearest and most complete presentation of that "glorious day" of our going to meet Him in the air!

And this word:

In progressive revelation we have all this data we can enter into our ever-growing picture of the Rapture.)

We are not finished with the accounts of the Rapture in my scroll called Revelation. We have seen the last trumpet sound; and we have seen the risen church in Heaven without fault or guile before the Heavenly throne; and many other wonderful descriptions given of those who were redeemed from the earth and from among men. However, we have not *'seen'* the actual Rapture yet.

But we will!

We still have to see the 'most striking scene of the Rapture' in my book. That wonderful scene is right on the horizon. It is the most picturesque scene of the Rapture in the entire Bible!

Keep reading.

10 + ONE

Nutshell Of Revelation 1-14

I began my scroll of 'the things which must come to pass' with a flat statement that I was in the spirit in the Lord's Day. As that trying time began I saw Jesus as the mighty One who would not let His churches (represented by seven of them in which He was in the midst) go without His protection thru the time of the tribulation alone.

Next I was taken to the Heavenly Control Center, the throne of God in Heaven. There the engaging event was the producing of a little scroll in God's right hand. I cried with the demand to find someone worthy enough to open the many seals on it and then to read it.

I wept greatly when no one could be found.

Jesus, the slain Lamb of God, soon came forward and was pronounced as the only one worthy to do the task of breaking the seven seals off it and of reading it. Catastrophic judgments on earth were triggered as the first six seals were broken. When the final seal was broken there was no judgment of any sort on earth.

The unsealed book was open in Jesus' hand and was ready to be read. However, in God's Game Plan the time of its reading was to follow the sounding of golden trumpets which had been offered to seven angels assembled before the throne. With each blowing there was a corresponding judgment on the earth.

The first four judgments were aimed at a 'third part of the earth.' The fifth trump gained renown by being much harsher in dimension and was therefore also called the FIRST WOE. The sixth was also massive in scope and was therefore the SECOND WOE.

The initial sounding of the last trumpet, when it first began to blow, brought the suffering Christians' salvation in the form of being raptured from the earth.

Before the throne of God in Heaven, they sang a NEW song which no man on earth could learn except the 144,000 Hebrews from the twelve tribes of Judah who had been gathered together on mount Zion with Jesus, as their redemptive Lamb, standing in their midst.

Now catch this.

Gospel Is Preached To All The World

At that point...with the true Christians home in Heaven and with the true Israelites home in mount Zion, I saw another angel fly in the midst of the heavens.

That angel was flying as a messenger of a direct 'promise' Jesus gave to us on the mount of Olives. There Jesus said that the gospel of the kingdom will be preached in all the world for a witness unto all nations and then should the end come.

In my visions I saw that this worldwide preaching in the air of the everlasting gospel (the good news of Jesus Christ will be the good news for all of eternity) by the FLYING ANGEL was the fulfillment of that very merciful promise. This proclamation came 'after the church was raptured' but before the trying time of wrath and of Jacob's trouble began. His preaching was in the right time sequence, friends, and, it was unto 'them that dwell on the earth, and to every nation, and kindred, and tongue and people.'

Back when our Lord Jesus was here on the earth with us He commissioned us to go and tell the whole world the good news of the gospel and we have attempted to do that. But, friends, I am very old and we still have not accomplished that command. Though we will never cease trying, maybe we never will. *This angel certainly is doing in one moment all that Jesus promised would be done. Even as the End is fast approaching, he presents the gospel to 'all the world for a witness unto all nations,' and then...and then...the end can come.*

Fear God: Worship God

His worldwide message: "Fear God, and give glory to Him. For the hour of His judgment IS come. Worship Him that made heaven and earth and sea and the fountains of waters."

It was then, and only THEN, after the seven seals had been broken off the scroll by Jesus, and, after those seven angels had sounded their golden trumpets **to announce the reading of that little scroll**, it was then, only then, that the angel also proclaims that the hour of His judgment IS come.

For the hour of His judgment IS come.

Those wicked men had it all wrong, back in the breaking of the sixth seal when they cried out in much terror: "For the great day of His wrath is come...."

No, no, wicked men can never tell us any of the timings of the Lord.

It is this angel in the sky who tells the entire world that the hour of God's judgment IS come. Remember, the twenty four elders had just claimed the same fact up in Heaven: "His wrath IS come."

(We claimed in the beginning of this book the first ten days of tribulation the church has to go through are NOT the days of the outpouring of the wrath of God. They are ten days of 'Great Tribulation'—see Rev. 2:10, 6:11 & 7:14—but the days are not any part of the time of the Father's wrath nor the hour of God's judgment nor of the time of Jacob's trouble.

Let's look at our new wine skin chart.

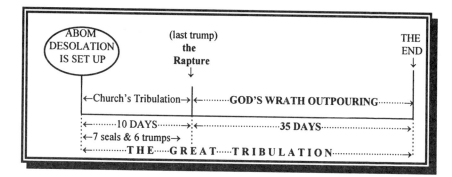

First, the **'Abomination of Desolation'** begins the Day of the Lord, i.e., the Lord's Day.

Second, the **Great Tribulation** begins.

Third, all people, the saved and the unsaved, are still HERE on the earth for the first ten days of that tribulation. During those ten days all people will experience the terrifying acts connected to the breaking of the seven seals and they will also experience the on-the-earth-events connected to the sounding of the seven trumpets–except that the church will leave the earth the instant the last trumpet begins to sound.

Fourth, the **'Rapture'** thus takes place.

Fifth, the Hour of Temptation begins and will last thirty-five days. Noah knew seven days before the rains were to begin that they would burst forth on the eighth day. I therefore believe the seal-breakings and the six trumpets will last for the first 7 days of the tribulation. Then probably 'late on the seventh day' the death of the two witnesses will occur; and therefore there will be a waiting through the eighth, the ninth and tenth days as those two lay in the streets. Early on the eleventh day, the two witnesses will rise upward and the great earthquake will occur, and soon after the Rapture will take place. That is one scenario of how the church will experience ten days of tribulation, and, then will rise in the Rapture sometime on the next day.

Also, all people, saved and unsaved, will hear the victorious shouts of 'Peace! Peace!' which will be believed, and will ring forth when those two witnesses are slain by the ultra-evil future dictator. The peoples of the world shall rejoice over the killings and shall make merry and shall send gifts one to another: because these two prophets had tormented them. Paul said when THEY SHALL SAY, PEACE AND SAFETY; then sudden destruction cometh upon them as travail upon a woman with child and they shall not escape.

The slaying of the two witnesses will begin the outcries of, 'Peace! and Safety! Peace! and Safety!' For three & a half days they will loudly proclaim those claims even while the 'demons out of the pit' continue their worldwide afflicting of all people with excruciating pain and while the armies of the East continue butchering off a third part of mankind.

However, **the climatic happening** which will CAUSE the wicked of this world to even more LOUDLY proclaim, 'Peace! and Safety, Peace! and Safety!' will be the Rapture of the church at the very beginning of the last trumpet on the eleventh day.

For, if the people of the world were rejoicing when the two were slain, what much greater rejoicing will proceed from their lips when all those *hideous* Christians *disappear and are out of their lives forever!*

They will not have any clue whatsoever as to where *'those Jesus-onlys'* went but they will be beyond themselves with joy!

"Peace and safety at last!" they will shout.

"PEACE!" and "SAFETY!"

Of course, THEN will come SUDDEN DESTRUCTION.)

Babylon Is Fallen

Cannot get much more 'sudden' that this! A second angel followed that first one, shouting:

Babylon is fallen!
Is fallen!

That great city has fallen because it made all nations drink of the wine of her fornication. I have much more to talk of on this also, however, I will wait for a more opportune time. I do want to get to the reading of the little scroll first.

A third angel followed the first two, shouting, *"If any man worships the beast and his image, and receives his mark in his forehead, or in his hand, the same shall drink of the wine of the wrath of God, which IS poured out without mixture into the cup of His indignation* (again it is only here that the wrath of God IS poured out...not earlier). *And he shall be tormented with fire and brimstone in the presence of the holy angels and in the presence of the Lamb* (what an awesome warning). *And the smoke of their torment will ascend up for ever and ever, and they have no rest day nor night* (who?), *who worship the beast and his image, and whosoever receives the mark of his name."*

That is heavy!

OH, IS THAT HEAVY!

See where greed is going to take many?

Is money and 'buying and selling' THAT important?

Every person on the face of this earth (the church of course has just been taken off) will hear that warning directly from the angel: *every person that accepts the mark of the beast will drink of the wine of the wrath of God and he shall be tormented...and he shall have no rest day or night for ever and ever.*

The warnings are all there.

BELIEF will again be the ultimate criteria.

Whom will they believe and trust.

I saw the patience of those saints: here are they that keep the commandments of God, and the faith of Jesus. These are those who would follow the Lord AFTER the church had been taken Home. Their requirements will be the same as ours.

There is no difference, is there?

The believers in the *hour of temptation* will have the same identification marks as do we Christians today.

THEN they will keep the commandments of God.

THEN they will keep the faith of Jesus.

And again, MANY will die for their stand.

I tell of those in my accounting of the first resurrection.

Note the three 'telling marks' of those believers who THEN die in the Lord: they are beheaded (1) for the witness of Jesus, and (2) for the word of God, and who (3) had not worshipped the beast, neither had received his mark.

Right AFTER the church's Rapture this worldwide warning against worshipping the beast & receiving the mark of his name is proclaimed. And from the first resurrection I saw that a large multitude will again follow our Lord even to death.

This angelic warning is also given after the sealed 144,000 Israelis have been gathered together with Jesus in their midst. It is they who have to be living in and inhabiting Israel when our Lord Jesus comes back to set up His reign over them, and over the rest of the world. He is in their midst to keep them safe for the Millennium.

Not ONE of those 144,000 Hebrew men and probably none of their wives or families will die during that tribulation time of Jacob's trouble.

Jesus will protect every last one of them.

You know that the coming wicked ruler would like to cause their death to be his first priority.

But just like Shadrach, Meshach, and Abednego in the fiery furnace...no man, and no fire and brimstone, will touch or harm these sealed followers of God!

The Longsuffering Mercy Of Our Father

Our Creator God and Father since before the foundation of this world has always looked out for His created beings. He has always looked out for all of mankind.

Always.

The scriptures are full of example after example.

Look at this one.

With the 'Christian and Jewish witness' out of reach for the world, His Game Plan has FOREVER included the sending of His angel to proclaim the message of hope and grace to all who are still upon the earth.

What hope do they have?

What hope do they have!

TONS OF HOPE–if they do not bow down and worship the

beast and its image. I have already told of those who after this will rise to life in the first resurrection. Just like the 'raptured' church which went before them to Heaven, these also lived and reigned with Him for 1000 years right here on the earth.

What a grand hope that will be!

The only thing is that those of us who go up in the Rapture, in the firstfruits harvest, are a special group to our Lord Jesus & His and our Father. We are the Bride of Christ. By all means... strive to be ready and waiting for Him when He comes to call us Home.

Be wise virgins with ready oil in your lamps.

Lord willing, the time is soon.

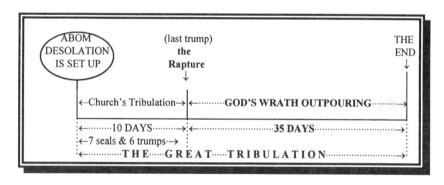

(From the above new wine skin chart, look at the 10 DAYS section. In those ten days of tribulation for the church we find the breaking of the seals and the sounding forth of the first six trumpets.

You will notice the arrow does not go all the way to the end of the ten days. For I feel that the activation of those events will be completed by the end of the 'seventh day.' The continuing effects of them will of course proceed into the rest of the 10 day period.

Also in those eighth, nineth and tenth days the two witnesses will lie in the streets.)

10 + TWO

Blessed Who Die Henceforth

And I heard a voice from Heaven saying unto me,

> ### *WRITE, BLESSED ARE THE DEAD WHICH DIE IN THE LORD FROM HENCEFORTH.*

Blessed are they who *'die in the Lord'* from henceforth, that is, FROM THE SEVENTH TRUMPET ONWARD.

That is, FROM THE RAPTURE ONWARD.

That is, blessed are those who *'die in the Lord'* during the terrifying pouring out of the wrath of God.

That is, blessed are those who *'die in the Lord'* during the reading of the little scroll.

That is, blessed are those who *'die in the Lord'* during the approximately thirty-five days until Jesus comes again!

That is, blessed are those who *'die in the Lord'* and have accepted the three worldwide warnings from the angels flying in the heavens.

The Father has EVERYTHING worked out.
Blessed are they who 'die in the Lord' henceforth!
HENCEFORTH, my friends!

The rapture has just taken place and immediately I was told that those who die in the Lord HENCEFORTH would be blessed. They will be blessed because they will partake in the 'first resurrection' and then they will also reign with our Lord Jesus with us!

The Father's Game Plan is awesome!

Awesome for everyone but not for the wicked. Woe to the wicked ones. We are going to read about them shortly, but first we are going to get a view of the Rapture taking place!

You heard me right!

Here is the Rapture taking place!

It Doesn't Get Any Better Than This

Or: here is the best of the best pictures of the Rapture in the entire Bible!

Is that not what this book is all about?

Is it not: The Revelation of Jesus Christ?

Is it not the book revealing Jesus in every role needed at the end time?

He is a slain Lamb.

He is the mighty One.

He is the Lord of the churches.

He is the only One worthy to open the book.

He is the Lion of the tribe of Judah.

He is the Root of David.

He is the One in the sixth trumpet sounding who swears by the Father as He lifted His hand to Heaven:

> *There shall be time no longer (for mankind to join His body). For ... in the days of the voice of the seventh angel (with the last trumpet), when he shall begin to sound, the mystery of God (the formation of the 'body of Christ' from Jews and Gentiles) shall be finished....*

He is the One who gives John the book to eat.

He is the Reaper of His own Body at the Rapture.

He is Israel's Lamb standing in their midst.

He is the coming Warrior-King on His white steed.

He is the One Who will destroy the beast and his co-hort, the false prophet.

He is the One Who will laid hold on Satan and bound him for a thousand years.

He is the One Who will reign for a thousand years.

He is the One Who with His Father will be the Temple of the New Jerusalem.

He is the One Who will be the light of that new city.

He is the One Who says:

> I Jesus have sent mine angel to testify
> unto you these things in the churches. I am
> the root and the offspring of David and the
> bright and morning star.

Jesus is truly the 'One' Whom my book of the End Times is all about throughout its entirety. Do not let any teacher ever give you the impression that it is about Satan and the beast and the false prophet. Oh they are in there...but...but only as minor characters.

It is God's Game Plan.

It is God's Prophetic Puzzle.

And, from cover to cover, it is about Jesus.

The Rapture Takes Place
in
Revelation 14:14-16

I looked, and behold a white cloud, and upon the cloud one sat like unto the Son of man! This is the first instance in those many Lord's Day scenes that I saw Jesus looking much like He looked that last time we saw Him before He was taken up into Heaven. This scene reminded me of the time with Peter and all in the boat when we saw Jesus on the shore up in Galilee after He rose from the grave. For then we were not quite sure that it was our Lord. We really hoped so, and thought so, but we were not quite sure...until we had been with Him for a little while.

In this scene I was again a little uncertain.

On His head He wore a golden crown and in His hand He held a sharp sickle. Therefore when He left His Father to descend to sit on the cloud, He was given His crown! He will be seen by His Bride as the conquering Monarch that He truly is.

An archangel rushed out of the temple in Heaven crying out with a loud voice to our Lord Jesus sitting on the cloud:

Thrust in Your sickle and reap! For the time IS come for You to reap! For the harvest of the earth IS ripe!"

Please understand what Jesus is being told to do here.

Please understand from where this angel has just come. It is in this scene that we see the Father telling the angel to go tell His Son that *the* **'day and hour'** *had finally come!*

That He could finally reap.

He could 'finally' thrust in His sickle and bring His bride Home! Once you see the truth of this scene, you will come back to it again and again and again.

And again and again.

I certainly think of it over and over.

And to think that it was given to me to write down.

Friends, this is the 'ONE SCENE' for which we have been looking in all the scriptures!

((This is the 'ONE SCENE' that progressive revelation holds up to us and says, See, here it is! All the scriptures point to and fit into THIS scene. Here is how all those scriptures will finally work out.))

Paul described the same scene prophetically.

**For the Lord Himself shall descend from
Heaven** (on a cloud) **with a shout, with the
voice of the archangel** (yelling, Thrust in
Your sickle!), **and with the trumpet of God**
(the last trumpet has just begun). **And the
dead in Christ shall rise first, then we
which are alive and remain shall be caught
up** (reaped by Him with His sickle) **together
with them in the clouds** (where He is at), **to
MEET THE LORD IN THE AIR and
so shall we ever be with the Lord!**
(I Thess.4:16-17.)

Paul also described it like this:

I show you a mystery.
We shall not all sleep (die). In a
moment, in the twinkling of an eye, at the
last trump (When the seventh trumpet begins
to sound forth). For the trumpet shall sound,
and, the dead shall be raised incorruptible,
and we (the living believing ones) shall be
changed! For this corruptible MUST
put on incorruption, and this mortal MUST
put on immortality!
(I Corinthians 15:51-53.)

The scene I saw was of the RAPTURE. It puts the finishing
touches on all the previous prophetic scriptures. It was what we
should look for in any End Times scroll the 'first time' we read
it. And to think it was given to me.

*('Progressive revelation' demands such a climatic scene of
Jesus taking us to Himself **in some nanosecond, eye-twinkling,
lightning-flashing manner.**)*

Here we discover the solution: in one gigantic sickle-sweep
Jesus will reap the entire planet of those who are watching and
waiting for Him. For the in that midheaven scene I saw:

He that sat on the cloud
thrust in His sickle on the earth;
and the earth was reaped!

The entire Earth was 'reaped' of its righteous followers of the Lamb of God. Friends, that is the RAPTURE in its foremost picturesque setting in all the scriptures!

Let Me Jump In Here For Awhile

That 'clear and complete,' most picturesque setting is right here in The Revelation of Jesus because that book is the only strictly-prophetic-book that is written expressly to the churches of Jesus Christ! And it is His LAST scriptural statement to His people everywhere.

The Revelation of Jesus is about:

	Jesus!	
Jesus!		*Jesus!*
	Jesus!	
Jesus!	*Jesus! Jesus! Jesus!*	*Jesus!*
Jesus!	*Jesus! JESUS! Jesus!*	*Jesus!*
Jesus!	*Jesus! Jesus! Jesus!*	*Jesus!*
	Jesus!	
Jesus!		*Jesus!*
	Jesus!	

The Revelation would have miserably failed the progressive revelation test if it had not come through with such a vivacious, outstanding and complete picture of our being harvested Home to Him. That vivid picture took place right before John's eyes!

The Revelation is not about Satan.

The Revelation is not about the Antichrist.

It says a little about each of them.

But the *'main'* and **'primary'** and *'overwhelming'* thrust throughout the sphere of the entire book is Jesus, Jesus, Jesus!

This is God's Game Plan!

And His Game Plan has ALWAYS been to bring glory to His dearly beloved Son!

Did We Not Promise This

Remember our word to you?

The Revelation is the most complete prophetic book in the New Testament and therefore we would also expect to find in it the clearest and most complete presentation of that future day when Jesus comes back to fulfill the PROMISE which He had given in **kernel-form** in that last evening with His disciples in the upper room when He informed them that He was leaving to prepare them a place, and that when He had finished He would come again to receive them unto Himself: that, where He was, they would also be.

And remember this word?

In this treatise of the book of Revelation that you are now holding in your hands you will be pleased to find *many plump passages describing convincing-further-details of our Lord's coming for us which will vividly present the final clear and complete presentation of the Rapture 'totally in accordance' with all the rapture scriptures presented up to that book.*

If we TRULY BELIEVE in progressive revelation then that is just what we would EXPECT to FIND in any position that is claiming to present a true picture of the time of the end.

And remember this word?

In progressive revelation we have all this data-wealth we can enter into our ever-growing picture of the Rapture. Friends, we are not yet finished with the accounts of the Rapture. We still have much to see and we will find all this and more in the book of Revelation.

A Son Is What He Is

One singular thought about **Jesus' Sonship** should not get away from us here. When the archangel came out of the temple in Heaven, and shouted, "THRUST in Your sickle and reap, for the time IS come for You to reap," that archangel was fulfilling one of the great wonders of the Godhead.

Please catch this. That was Jesus' *wonderful willingness to always be a Son to His Father*. Always. We find it all the way through the Gospels. All the way through. And in the Proverbs many believe that Jesus was speaking when *wisdom* said:

> *Then I was by Him, as One brought up with Him: and I was daily His delight, rejoicing always before Him.*

Jesus was, and still is, a 'SON' to His Father in relation to how, and when, things should be done. When it came to Jesus' death, He knew it would be some Passover because the *type* in that instance was too perfect: He knew He had come to die for the sins of the people *even as the unblemished lambs were to be slain for the sins of their people*. Thus He knew it would be some Passover when He would also die—but He did not know which one.

He completely left that 'time-decision' up to His Father. Completely. That is why John records in 13:1, "Now before the feast of the passover, WHEN Jesus KNEW THAT HIS HOUR WAS COME that He should depart out of this world unto the Father...."—John is stating here that an *'assurance'* came to Jesus that the time had come. It was a 'knowing' which Jesus had not had nor had displayed at any of the other Passovers He had attended.

Certainly the PRECISE TIMIMG of His death had been left totally up to the pleasure and purpose of His Father.

Along this line, another puzzling statement of His affirmed: "But of that day and hour knows no man,...not the angels which are in Heaven, NEITHER THE SON, but the Father."

He thus made it clear that only the Father knew the *day and hour* of Jesus' coming again to get us.

That was perfectly fine with Jesus.

He was the Son.

And will always be the Son.

The Son was not the Boss.
The Father is the Boss.

He therefore made the startling assertion that even though He knew He had come to die—He did not know the exact time when He would—until the Word came to Him from His Father. Now again He makes the startling claim that even He does not know the precise time (the day and hour) in which He was to return. Only the Father would give the Word that the time had come. He was the SON.

He was the Son, friends.

Only the Father would declare when the time had come for Him to bring His Bride Home. Sure ... He was anxious to bring all His followers Home. Sure ... He had all the ability needed to just go ahead with that reaping of the Earth. But, no, NO WAY would He not wait for the Word from His Father. It is the cloud scene in The Revelation which explains how it will happen.

On the correct day, Jesus will descend on a cloud. He will have a sickle in His hand. However, He will not go ahead and reap. The timing of the reaping is STILL in His Father's control.

So He will sit there and wait.
He is ready.
He knows the day has come.
He even has the crown on His head.

But, as an obedient Son who truly loves His Father, He waits. (Even as He waited when He had broken the seven seals off that little scroll. He did not proceed with that reading. He waited for the word from His Father, and when instead the seven angels were given those seven golden trumpets He still continued to wait.)

He is the Son.
His Father is the Boss.

> *Suddenly, the wait is over!*
> *Suddenly, the hour is come!*
> *The Father has given the word!*
> *And when He says, "GO!"*
>
> *THE ANGEL FLIES OUT OF THE TEMPLE AND*
> *SHOUTS TO THE SON ON THAT WHITE CLOUD,*
> *"Thrust in Your sickle and reap, FOR THE TIME IS*
> *COME"*
>
> *For the time HAS come.*

Don't tell us that Jesus NOW knows the time.
Revelation tells us that He STILL does NOT know.
The Father will tell Him the time through the angel.
That's where Paul's 'voice of the archangel' comes in:

For the Lord Himself shall descend
from heaven with a shout, with
the voice of the archangel....

What a Savior we have!

What a Husband we are going to be going Home to!

If you are the independent type...cultivate depending on the Lord in your remaining days here on the earth. For as He is *'a prefect Son,'* so He will want us to be *'His perfect wife.'* And wives are not to boss their Husband.

We all need to learn from Him.

The point is...here at the sounding of the last trumpet in The Revelation...Jesus is seen clearly 'WAITING' for the DECREE from His Father to reap...for His Father had made it abundantly clear that He would decide the moment.

When the archangel shouts to the Son to reap. At that same instant the seventh (last) angel IS ordered to begin sounding his trumpet. Thus, the sweetness comes first in God's Game Plan's time of wrath. Then the thirty-five days of wrath. But first....

10 + THREE

Abraham, His Servant, And Isaac

The three above people are *'types'* for us to look at now that we have seen the Rapture in the Revelation. We have all seen *types* in our sacred scriptures which are extremely true to the historical event which happens later. Of course Jesus refers to the days of Noah and Lot as good examples *(types)* of the days of His coming again.

With that in mind, in Genesis we find that 'father' Abraham 'represents' our Heavenly Father when Abraham takes his only son (interesting that God called Isaac his *'only'* son) up Mount Moriah and is willing to offer his son's life there upon an altar. Abraham foreshadows (represents) what the Father would one day be willing to do to His only Son on that SAME mountain.

Abraham was the Father in *'type'*.

Isaac was Jesus in *'type'*.

In the next chapter Abraham's wife died (which SETS the scene for the following chapter. For in the Godhead there is NO woman or wife. At first there was only God Almighty. Then He decided to bring forth a Son from WITHIN Himself WHO also would have 'every attribute' that He Himself had—we call that action cloning today. Thus way back in eternity God Almighty brought forth His *firstborn*—and His *only-begotten—Son* from WITHIN Himself. Later...the Holy Spirit 'proceeded forth' also from WITHIN the Father. Thus They are all of One ESSENSE.

They all have the same attributes; that is, They are all 'GOD' in totality...yet that First One is *God Almighty*. The Second is *His Son*. The Third is *His Holy Spirit*. No female was needed. And no female is in Their Godhead.

The Father, the Son, and the Holy Spirit are represented in the holy scriptures as INDIVIDUAL MEMBERS making up the Godhead. The Father is always the Most High. Jesus is always the Son. The Spirit is always the Spirit of God or the Spirit of Christ.)

Genesis 24: "Abraham was old." Therefore he calls his eldest servant (soon seen as a *type* of the Holy Spirit) and says to him:

> *Go unto my country, and to my kindred,*
> *and take a wife unto my son Isaac.*
>
> *Take not my son to that far country again.*
> *A wife you shall take unto my son from thence.*

The far country to which his son is not go to AGAIN to get a bride is obviously *in type* this Earth. Jesus is not to come here again to get His bride, the church.

The servant departed to Abraham's former land even as the Holy Spirit was *sent here* AFTER Jesus had left—for it was expedient for Jesus *to leave* so the Holy Spirit could come (and through the years gather a Bride for Him).

In the intriguing narrative the servant is 'led' to a 'perfect bride' for Issac. A young virgin named Rebekah. In *'type'* that young maiden represents the church, the bride of Christ.

Rebekah runs home to tell her family that a servant of their relative Abraham has come!

They invite him in.

The servant shares his mission with them:

> *My master made me swear, saying,*
> *thou shall not take a wife to my son of the daughters*
> *of the Canaanites. But you shall go to my kindred,*
> *and take a wife unto my son.*

In his recounting of his meeting Rebekah, he shares that he was enthralled by her **'willingness'** to come to this stranger's assistance. Also in that she turned out to be an actual relative of his master Abraham's (of course, which was one of Abraham's prerequisites.)

So they answer him:

> ### *Take her and go and let her*
> ### *be your master's son's wife.*

As soon as the servant knew that she was going to accept becoming his master's son's wife, he lavished upon her MANY many gifts. In *type* the Holy Spirit lavishes on us His gifts here on earth...even as with the servant He does not wait until He has taken us home. Here is where we need the gifts of the Holy Spirit.

When the family naturally wanted her **'departure'** to be delayed for a little while longer, the servant said that he should be returning with the bride-to-be.

The family called Rebekah, and asked:

> ### *Will you go with this man?*

> ### *She said, "Yes."*

And we read:

> ### *the servant took Rebekah*
> ### *and went his way.*

In *type* the believers also have to respond with a **YES** to the question, "Will you go with this Man (will you 'accept Jesus as your Lord and Master' and go wherever His Spirit leads)?"

NOW...NOW catch this.

Even as that servant (the Holy Spirit) is taking her back to Abraham's (God's) country, ISAAC (Jesus) HAS LEFT HIS FATHER'S HOME and, out in a field (out on the white cloud), he lifts up his eyes and sees Rebekah coming with his servant.

And we read:

> *Isaac brought her home,*
> *and she became his wife,*
> *and he loved her.*

That was the only reason Isaac was out in the field.

He was not there with the intent to 'leave' his father and go *again* to that far country. Even so with Jesus, He goes down to that white cloud for only ONE reason, He does not 'go' there with the intent to 'leave' His Father and 'go' AGAIN to that far country, the Earth. No, not at that time before He gets His Bride.

Jesus also leaves His Father, and comes down to sit on one of our clouds, and receives His Bride as the Spirit brings us up to Him on the cloud. And Jesus will then also take us back up into His Home as His bride. For that is THE ONLY reason HE comes downward to sit on the white cloud in our skies. To meet us *out in the field* with the full INTENT to return immediately back up to His Home in Heaven.

To Meet The Lord In The Air

Remember how Paul wrote it:

> *Then we which are alive and remain*
> *shall be 'caught up togeher with them' in the clouds,*
> *to meet the Lord in the air and so shall*
> *we ever be with the Lord.*

Jesus descended to that cloud with that sharp sickle in His hand with just one purpose in mind. **To reap the earth** (that is, the 'far country' to which He was forbidden to go back to get Himself a bride) **of His followers, of His bride.**

Two other times is the word meaning 'to meet' found in the New Testament. In Matt.25:6, the bridegroom comes, meets the five *'ready'* virgins and *'proceeds' to the marriage feast*. He comes with the express purpose of gathering those virgins who are ready for his coming, and then he proceeds to take them to the marriage feast.

In Acts 28:15, Paul is traveling to Rome, on his journey the brethren hear of his coming and rush out to *'meet'* him. At that point they go with Paul WHERE he is going.

* All three meetings are not the destination places.

* All three meetings are for the **main person** to take those who come TO WHERE HE IS GOING.

Jesus 'meets' believers in the clouds to take them up to His Home to be wedded to them. He is not upon the cloud with the intent to reap the earth of His bride and then to bring them back *down here*. He is there to take them *back Home to His Father* with Him.

The bridegroom 'meets' the five ready virgins expressly to take them with him *to the wedding feast*.

The brethren 'meet' Paul and go with him *to 'where' he is going. That is, to Rome.*

Do not let any teach you that Jesus is descending to the earth, and, that on the way He meets us in the mid-air, and He then continues downward to the earth with us. *He descends to the cloud with one distinct purpose in mind. He wants to reap His followers to Him so that He can take them back up Home with Him.*

The Son is out in the 'field' but He is not the One Who is in control as to the timing of when His 'Rebekah' is going to be coming to Him. Jesus is not there for the purpose of continuing on to our planet. He is there for one purpose: to harvest our old rotating planet of His bride and then to take her back to Heaven with Him.

Missionary C.T. Studd

What an example of one sold out to our Lord. My copy of *C.T. Studd* by Norman P. Grubb is so tattered by reading and re-reading and re-reading and underlining that it has to be held together by rubber bands. I have a newer edition of the book but I love that first copy.

Studd was one who in today standards gave away millions of heir-money on his twenty-first birthday so that he could be a follower of Jesus to his utmost.

How will our Lord judge him and the early disciples who also left ALL to follow Him, and...also judge the vast majority who seemingly leave almost nothing to follow Him.

What a dilemma.

In Psalms 40, Jesus, in that pre-New Testament prophetic scripture, gives us a much different design of 'seeing' where we stand with the Lord:

> *"Sacrifice and offering You did not desire," He*
> *says to His Father. Stating that they were the end*
> *results of disobedience. The Father wants obedience*
> *instead. He adds, "Burnt offering and sin offering*
> *You have not required," making it even clearer.*

Then Jesus shares a personal testimony of what His Father desires and requires:

> *"Lo, I come...I delight to do Your will,*
> *O my God." Simply put, we do what He asks us*
> *to do and we show Him our love to Him.*

When I read of C.T.Studd and all his spiritual surrenders, I am reminded of that above saying of Jesus.

Those whose lives observe and do the above will rise when Jesus swings that sickle of His. They will rise upward to meet Him where He waits for them. They are 'followers' of Him wheresoever He leads. Of course none of us has that *Son-desire* which Jesus exhibited when He was here no matter where we live on this old planet.

But Jesus did.

Never did He need offerings and sacrifices.

Never.

He has told us no matter where we live that He will live as the *'Resident Boss'* in our lives if we invite Him to do so. He would love to daily LIVE on the throne of our life and cause us to live a life that shouts forth: "I delight to do Your will, O my God."

In ourselves we can't and won't do that.

But *in Him*, He can and has (when He was here on earth as 'Jesus of Nazareth'), and, therefore, He can in each one of our hearts which asks Him to LEAD us in such a way that He truly is the Boss of our lives...then, friends, we will delight to do our Father's will daily.

So the dilemma is answered.

'WE' live in control of our lives wherever we live and WE will need an abundance of 'forgiveness' and 'sacrifices' and 'offerings'...*OR we allow HIM the control of our lives and we will see that sin offerings are not 'required' of us as long as He is in control. He will live a life in us that delights in the will of the Father.*

If we will allow Him the control of our lives. Of course first we accept His complete 'sacrifice' of Himself for our sins and disobediences...then we all have the opportunity of having Him live in us as 'Resident Boss'.

He does...and we will please the Father.

He does not...and we will soon displease the Father.

All too soon.

And all too often.

The choice is ours to make: no matter 'where' we live, no matter what 'culture' we live in, no matter how rich or poor we are, no matter what any of our circumstances are.

The Last Trump Of God

The seven announcing trumpets certainly give us a new **set** to consider as we attempt to decide which last trumpet Paul was referring to in his promise:

> *Behold I show you a mystery...*
> *In a moment, in the twinkling eye,*
> *at the last trump*

* * Jesus was seen in the midst of the churches.
* * Seven stern warnings were given to the churches.

* * One warning said specifically that the 'faithful' church would go through ten days of tribulation–they would suffer and they were exhorted to be faithful until death.

* * In the breaking of the fifth seal all those martyrs were slain for the word of God, and the testimony which they held. They were told to wait a little season until their fellow-servants and their *'brethren'* were also killed. They certainly had all the marks of being true Christians.

* * In the sixth seal more brethren were also taken Home for the same reasons. Both of the groups sound like those who were *'faithful unto death'* from up above.

* * Thus, a literal reading of the events of this story would lead us to believe that all these 'believers' are indeed of the true church which thus HAS NOT BEEN RAPTURED at that point in the book.

Before he saw the rapture, John was told by a Messenger (who was most likely Jesus) AFTER the sixth trumpet had been sounded and had run its course:

> *In the days of...the seventh angel, when he*
> *shall begin to sound, the mystery of God (the mystery*
> *was the forming together of Jew and Gentile into one*
> *body in which dwelt 'Christ in you':so wrote*
> *Paul) should be finished. "*

That Messenger who seemed to be Jesus said that in the very (spilt-second) beginning of the sounding of the last of the seven golden trumpets, the 'completion' of the building of the body of Christ should be finished.

Before He said these words, He said that there was time no longer. That is that *there was no longer time for anyone to repent and accept the gospel and to enter into the only body of people who would become the Bride of our Lord Jesus.*

John wrote graphically:

> *I looked, and behold a white cloud, and upon the cloud one sat like unto the Son of man, having on His head a golden crown, and in His hand a sharp sickle*
> *Another angel came out of (God's Heavenly Temple) crying with a loud voice to Him that sat on the cloud.*
> *"Thrust in Your sickle and reap! For the time has come for You to reap! For the harvest of the earth is ripe!"*

The time has come. Jesus is told to reap. For the harvest of the earth IS ripe. Jesus reaps.

Jesus said that He did not know of the day and the hour. To that coming moment on the white cloud, He still does not know the day and hour. As always...He leaves those decisions in the Father's hand! He just sits on the cloud waiting.

Waiting for the command of His Father to reap.

Waiting for the voice of the archangel to inform Him of His Father's demand to reap. Waiting, because He has always left the exact timing of the Rapture up to His Father.

Having always left *the timing of every important action* up to His Father, our Lord Jesus is the perfect example of a Son whose highest calling is to be obedient.

Ever anxious to bring us Home to Himself, Jesus descends and waits in our heavens on a cloud for that shout, 'the voice of the archangel.'

This harvesting that John saw done by Jesus was **NEVER** foreshadowed anywhere back in His teachings in the Gospels. Paul presented all the details of it...but even he never called it a reaping.

In Jesus' parables of the 'end of this age' *only angels* do the reaping. Therefore the first reaping by the angels He referred to, the harvest of the tares, is the next subject of John's Revelation.

The Three Good Reapings

Before we look at the tares-harvesting, let's summerize the three reapings of the 'good'. Of course, the first was the one by Jesus that we have just rehearsed. Jesus' Bride, though they are a part of the good seed, were reaped Home by Jesus Himself, so they are not included in this famous angelic *'end of the age'* harvesting.

A second 'reaping' of the good will be accomplished by the first resurrection. Neither of those two harvestings refer to the one mentioned in the parable in Matthew thirteen. But they are genuine 'gatherings' of large groups of good seed. Still, there is the Jesus-identified group of good seed who will feel the glory of God's grace and mercy in the millennium.

The first two just mentioned will reign with Jesus.

The last group will not reign with Christ at all.

Like the first two groups, the last will not bow down and worship the beast in the Hour of Temptation. However, they do not receive Jesus as LORD either. They don't therefore die for their 'faith' of Jesus. However, they are *very important* people across the world in that *they befriend (1) the church believers in the ten days of their suffering, and, then they befriend (2) those who in the period after the rapture come to a faith in Jesus.*

Matthew Twenty-Five

Matthew **24** twenty-four is all about the End Times, and you know that all of Matthew **twenty-five** was also only about the time of the end.

First Jesus shares two 'kingdom of heaven' parables.

Then He talks about when He comes again in His glory to reign upon the throne of His glory. At that point angels shall gather all nations before him. (Those are the 'good seed' which the angels shall gather *LAST* into the barns *AFTER* they have gathered the TARES prior to this for judgment.)

Those gathered good-seed nations will be separated into two groups.

The sheep.

The goats.

They have made it through Jacob's trouble. However, the sheep group *did something* during that time for which Jesus is going to reward them. (He again shows how much He wants people to live and enjoy this world He and His Father have created for us.) To them He says:

> *Come, you blessed of My Father, inherit the*
> *kingdom prepared for you from the*
> *foundation of world.*

Why does He tell the sheep that?

Why does He not tell the goats that?

He goes on to say that when He was hungry, when He was thirsty, when He was a stranger, when He was naked, and when He was sick, and when He was in prison *'those'* on His right hand—*the sheep*—catered to all of His wants.

Having become righteous people, the sheep ask Him **WHEN** they had done these things for Him.

They know they had never done anything for Him.

He gives a very short answer.

A short answer which brings tears to each and everyone of them as they stood before Him.

Tears of gratitude.

Tears of realizing that SOMEONE HAD seen them doing right. He IS a *just* and *righteous* King, they think.

His answer proved that to them:

> *Inasmuch as you have done it (any of the*
> *above friend-type deeds He has just named) unto*
> *one of the least of THESE MY BRETHREN,*
> *you have done it unto Me.*

How else are Jesus' Christian brethren-believers going to make it through those first ten days of tribulation?

How else are those in the wrath-group going to be able to survive up UNTIL the time they KNEW they were going to be beheaded in the hour of temptation?

Millions upon millions of people around this old globe knew these BRETHREN of Jesus were the 'good guys'—*even if they were not going to accept their beliefs.* Therefore they RISKED

MUCH to *befriend* them, *for it was in their nature to do so.*

God was working in them—and they too, like Thomas, and like the 144,000, would accept the truth of Jesus in the end. Even if it was by sight, and not faith.

These are the RIGHTEOUS ONES who will *repopulate* the entire world along with the 144,000 Jewish families for the final thousand years of this planet's existence.

Of course there were those who were not going to befriend anybody but themselves; those who were not going to get into trouble helping people with whom they didn't even believe the same things. Jesus said to those goats:

> *Inasmuch as you did it not to one of the least of these, you did it not to Me. Depart from Me, you cursed, into everlasting fire...*

Back To John's Revelation

Another angel came out of the temple in Heaven.

He also having a sharp sickle.

And another archangel came out from the altar, and cried to him, saying, Thrust in your sickle and gather the clusters of the vine of the earth; for her grapes are fully ripe.

The angel obeyed and gathered the vine and cast it into the great winepress of the wrath of God.

So, after the Rapture of the church, we have the gathering of the TARES into the Great Winepress of the wrath of God. At this point they are being harvested for judgment, but of course not for their ultimate judgment.

That will come soon enough.

Matthew 13:38-42

(Jesus taught concerning this reaping:

The field is the world...the tares are the children of the wicked one. The enemy that sowed them is the devil; the harvest is the end of the world (age); and the reapers are the angels (notice that Jesus' reaping is not in this story). As therefore the tares are gathered and burned in the fire; so shall it be in the end of this world. The Son of man shall send forth His angels and they shall gather out of His kingdom all things that offend, and them which do inquity; and shall cast them into a furnace of fire: there shall be wailing and gnashing of teeth."

In The Revelation, we are in the beginning moments of that unfortunate scene concerning the 'TARES' of this world. But, friends, they are tares because they have chosen to be tares.

They are 'tares' because they have chosen to be children of the evil one.

Our God and Father has presented to them every reason to leave their wicked ways but they LOVE disobedience and they love their freedom which is not freedom at all.

But to them they think addiction and slavery to all kinds of drugs and addiction and slavery to all kinds of mis-behaving is 'freedom'.

Having eyes to see, they are blind.
Blinded by the god of this world.
They do not see it.

They are *'blind'* to their slavery.

They are *'blind'* to what their life-styles are doing to their bodies and to themselves.

They are *'blind'* to the wonders of living a joyful life which is dedicated to following the Lord withersoever He leads.

And they are *'blind'* to their future.)

The Seven Vials Of Wrath

Another seven angels came forth in Heaven. They had the seven last plagues. LAST for in them **IS** FILLED UP the wrath of God.

Before the seven plagues are cast forth, the assembled risen church breaks forth with song:

> **Great and marvellous are Your works,**
> **Lord God Almighty!**
> **Just and true are Your**
> **ways thou King of saints.**
>
> **Who shall not fear You, Lord, and glorify**
> **Your name? For You are holy: for all nations**
> **shall come and worship before You; for Your**
> **judgments are made manifest.**

The angels stepped forth clothed in pure and white linen and golden girdles. One of the four heavenly creatures gave to them seven golden vials FULL OF THE WRATH OF GOD.

The Heavenly Temple was filled with smoke from the glory of God and from His power and no man was able to enter into the Temple, till the seven plagues are fulfilled.

The Seven Plagues

* Noisome and grievous sores were sent upon the men who had the mark of the beast and on them which worshipped his image.

* The sea became as the blood of dead men and every living soul died in the sea.

* The rivers and fountains of waters became blood.

> *The angel of the waters cried,*
> *"You are righteous, Lord...because You*
> *have judged thus. For they have shed the blood of saints and*
> *prophets: You have given them blood to drink."*
>
> *And another cried, "Even so, Lord God Almighty, true*
> *and righteous are Your judgments."*

* The sun was given power to SCORCH men with fire, with

great heat. The men were scorched and they BLASPHEMED the name of God which has power over these plagues, and they REPENTED NOT to give Him glory.

* The Beast's kingdom became full of darkness and the men in it gnawed their tongues for pain. And they BLASPHEMED the God of Heaven because of their pains, and their sores, and they REPENTED NOT of their deeds.

* The great river Euphrates dried up so that the way of the kings of the east 'might be prepared' (to go to Jerusalem to do battle). When that occurs, Satan, and the Beast (Antichrist), and the false prophet send miralce-working messengers to the kings of the earth (on their side) to gather them to the battle of the GREAT DAY OF GOD ALMIGHTY. And God gathered them all together into the valley of Armageddon.

* A great voice cried out of the Temple:

"IT IS DONE!"

The cry was followed by a cascading of voices, thunders and lightnings! A great earthquake—far greater than any since men were upon the face of the earth—divided Rome into three parts, and the great cities of the nations fell!

Every island disappear!

The mountains cannot be found! And, there fell great size hail out of heaven...and the men BLASPHEMED God for all the plagues, but especially because of that final plague of hail; for that plague was exceeding great.

The Judgment Of Mystery Babylon

It's back to me again.

Having presented the pouring forth of the 'wrath' of God which filled up the seven golden vials, John focused in on the beast (the nation of the Antichrist & the Antichrist himself) and upon the Whore, who sits upon many waters and upon that beast, whom he describes as the great city which reigns over the kings of the earth. In his time, Rome thus reigned.

The beast-kingdom is an interesting ONE. Of course IT IS present today. There is no mistaking it. I have much to write on it. Much. But most of that will go into a follow-up book to this one. I do that for two reasons: One, I want all to see that The Revelation is PRIMARILY about our Lord Jesus and so I don't want to dwell on these other lesser characters; and, two, to write about the beast, and the whore, and the others will force us to enter into much speculation.

I do not want 'speculating' to become the *'FOCUS'* of this book. I don't want people to dismiss the logical conclusions of this edition simply because some speculation I present does not come about as I have stated it might.

At the right time speculating is very important. For we are told and we are warned to WATCH.

Having said that about this study, I will come out with a speculative book soon for all to consider. For that is all we can do with speculation...consider its possibilities.

Period.

Did you notice that in 18:2 the message is clear to all who read: Babylon the great is fallen. And the system that is being referred to there is a worldwide one. 17:1 and 15.

Therefore in 18:4, even though the great city is fallen, since it is a worldwide system, at that point all her people are urged to:

**Come Out Of Her, My People,
That You Be Not Partakers Of Her Sins,
And That You Receive Not Of Her Plagues.**

**How Much She Has Glorified Herself, And
Has Lived Deliciously, So Much Torment
And Sorrow Give Her: For She Says In
Her Heart, I Sit A Queen, And Am
No Widow, And Shall See No
Sorrow**

Many of God's people are in her and the day is coming when

when a voice out of Heaven will urge the leaving of her.

That voice is future.

But all will need to heed it when it sounds forth.

A Couple Interesting Timings

We should notice that in ONE DAY her plagues will come: death and mourning and famine and she will be utterly burned with fire, for "strong is the Lord God who judges her."

Once one sees the new 'wine skin' chart with its short 35 days of the pouring out of the wrath of God, then, for us to see that her judgment is going to occur all in *one day* makes a lot of sense.

Not only will it occur in *one day,* but in **one hour** of that one day: "...great riches *will* come to nought...every shipmaster, and all the company in ships, and sailors, and as many as trade by sea, stood afar off and cried when they saw the smoke of her burning, saying, what city is like unto this great city!"

Her destruction has to come: "...for her merchants were the great men of the earth; for by HER sorceries were ALL nations deceived. And in her was found the blood of prophets, and of saints, and of all that were slain upon the earth."

Another One Hour Judgment

Back in 17:12, an unique statement is made: "The ten **10** horns which you saw are **10** kings (most believe 'Europe' is the continent and the revived empire envisioned here) who receive power as kings *one hour* with the beast."

The extremely short time period is remarkably significant because the nations of Europe have **NEVER** been able to unite together *as say the USA and the USSR were able to do.* But for one hour, and only *one hour,* they will unite with the beast!

When it says 'one hour' I believe it means *one hour.*

And we know precisely when that 'one hour' will be.

It will occur after the three wicked 'godhead' (Satan, the Antichrist, and the false prophet) send forth the miracle-working messengers to the kings of the earth to join forces with them in Israel.

Naturally, Europe's will be the last kings to join up with the beast. They will come at the LAST HOUR.

But, have no doubt about it, they will come.

For ONE HOUR.

And then....

10 + FOUR

Jesus Comes To Destroy Those
Who Are Destroying The Earth

What a wonderful chapter to which we have come!
John, go ahead.
After all that occurred on the Earth in the pouring out of the
seven golden vials full of wrath and with all that happened to the
great city called Mystery Babylon, I heard a great voice of much
people in Heaven, saying,

Alleluia! Salvation, and glory, and honour,
and power, unto the Lord our God! For true and
righteous are His judgments: for He has judged
the great whore, which did corrupt the earth
with her fornication, and (He) has avended the
blood of His servants at her hand.

Her smoke rose up for ever and ever.
The twenty-four elders and the four creatures fell down and
worshipped God sitting on His throne, saying:

Amen!
Alleluia!

Another voice came out of the throne, saying:

Praise our God, all you His servants,
and you that fear Him, both small and great!

I heard the Bride Herself also as it were the voice of a great multitude, and as the voice of many waters, and, as the voice of mighty thunderings, saying:

Alleluia: for the Lord God Omnipotent reigns!
Let us be glad and rejoice, and give honour to Him,
for the marriage of the Lamb IS come, and
His wife has made herself ready!

I saw His beaming bride as arrayed in fine linen, clean and white, for the fine linen is the righteousness of saints. And the voice said to me:

Write: Blessed are they which are called
to the marriage supper of the Lamb.

When he added, These are the true sayings of God. A thought hit me that I should show some sort of homage to him and I fell at his feet to worship him."

"NO," he shouted. "See that you do not do it! I am your fellow-servant, and of your brethren that have the testimony of Jesus. 'Worship God, John': for the testimony of Jesus is the spirit of prophecy."

Then....

Then....

Then I saw Heaven opened!

Behold I saw a white horse!

And HE THAT SAT UPON HIM was called:

+ + + **F A I T H F U L** ++ +   **and**   + + + + **T R U E !** + ++ +

In righteousness He judges and makes war.

His eyes were as flames of fire!

On His head were many crowns!

He had a name written which no man knew, it was known only by Jesus Himself!

He was clothed with a vesture dipped in blood.

His name is called:

The Word of God

The armies of Heaven which followed Jesus rode on white horses. They were clothed in fine linen, white and clean.

Out of His mouth I saw a sharp sword, with it He would smite the nations. He would rule the nations with a rod of iron. He was going to tread the winepress of the fierceness and wrath of Almighty God, His Father.

The last thing I saw was a name written on His vesture and on His thigh:

KING OF KINGS
AND
LORD OF LORDS

Oh, the glory of it all! Glory! I could have wished for those moments to have gone on and on. I was so taken back by His beauty. By His awesomeness! By the genuine magnificence of every detail I was beholding! But an angel, standing in the sun, cried aloud to all the fowls which fly in the midst of heaven:

Come and gather yourselves together unto the supper of the great God! That you may eat the flesh of kings, and the flesh of captains and the flesh of mighty men, and the flesh of horses and of them that sit on them, and the flesh of all men, both free and bond, both small and great.

The Taking Of The Beast And The False Prophet

Next I saw the beast, and the kings of the earth, and the vast hordes of their armies. They were a massive multitude that filled the entire valley and plains called Armageddon. The hosts waited as if they were invincible.

They were not.

The battle went easily and quickly to our Lord of Lords and our King of Kings. The beast was captured and with him the false prophet which had worked all manners of miracles before him. Great miracles with which he had deceived them that had received the mark of the beast and them which had worshipped his image.

The beast and his false prophet were thrown alive into the lake of fire burning with brimstone. The remnant of the kings & of their armies were slain with the sword of Him Who sat upon the horse, which sword proceeded out of His mouth.

Great Supper Of God

The fowls were filled with the flesh of His enemies and that was of course the great supper of God. It was **great** for the vast numbers of the victims slain. It was **'of God'** because He had ordained it and gave it.

That supper upon the earth is in *'antithesis'* to the happy marriage supper of the Lamb (and the Bride) which will be a most joyous 'celebration-occasion'. The fowl's 'great supper' is the same supper those fowls are called to participate in Ezekiel 39:17ff where we read:

> *Speak unto every feathered fowl, and to every*
> *beast of the field, Assemble yourselves, and come;*
> *gather yourselves on every side to My sacrifice that I*
> *do sacrifice for you, even a great sacrifice upon the*
> *mountains of Israel, that you may eat flesh*
> *and drink blood.*
>
> *You will eat the flesh of the mighty and drink*
> *the blood of the princes of the earth...you shall eat*
> *till you be full and drink blood till you be drunken*
> *of My sacrifice which I have sacrificed for you.*

> *Thus will you be filled at My table with*
> *horses and chariots, with mighty men, and with*
> *all men of war, saith the Lord GOD.*

In the battle that provided this great supper of God for those fowls of the air, Jesus' army will not suffer a casualty, and the enormous united armies of all the Western world ... plus the massive armies of the far north and of the Far East ... will be utterly defeated. Those enemies' *remains* will still be found and buried seven months into the millennium! (Ezek.39:11-16.) And the vast array of the enemies' weapons will be found and burnt as late as seven years into the millennium! (Ezek.39: 9-10.)

Ezekiel was writing about the far northern countries (Gog, Magog, etc.) when he gave those figures of months and years, but I am convinced that those numbers will also include all the bones and weapons of all the 'kings of the earth' which battle against our Lord Jesus that fateful day.

After that final battle ... when Jesus sets up His kingdom in Jerusalem there will not be a 'new heaven and a new earth' at that time. Those don't exist until a thousand years later.

When He sets up His throne and His kingdom in Judaea, the people under Him will not have it 'rosey-rosey' like Adam and Eve had it in the garden. No, no, no, the citizens under our Jesus will have all kinds of clean up and starting over to do.

However, they will have Jesus as King to lead them in that glorious task. I hope you realize that even the Third Temple will not be completed until *years* after His thousand year reign (the Millennium) begins. *Daniel was shown the Temple would not be completely built and cleansed by the priests till a period of two thousand and three hundred days (2,300 days)* after *that depraved transgression of destruction (the Abomination of Desolation) was set up.*

That is, Jesus will not oversee the final completion of that Third Temple which will be followed by its 'priestly cleansing' for service UNTIL well into the seventh year of His reign.

Let me repeat that:

Jesus will not oversee the final completion of the Third Temple which will lead up to its cleansing for service until well into the seventh year of His reign.

King Jesus comes to defeat His enemy on the forty-fifth **(45)** day after the Abomination of Desolation takes place. Thus we subtract 45 days from 2300 days ... and get a difference of 2255 days. Six years times 360 days a year is 2160 days. Thus Jesus' Temple will be cleansed for service ninety-five **95** days into the seventh year of the millennium.

That is very concordant with what the Bible tells us of how long it took King Solomon to build the First Temple back in his time. Even with having almost all the material gathered for him by his father David, Solomon was still "seven years in building the first temple." I Kings 6:38.

What a day it was when it was completed and cleansed!

What a day it will be when Jesus' Temple is completed!

Here's what happened when Solomon's was:

> *Now when Solomon had made an end of praying, the fire came down from heaven, and consumed the burnt offering and the sacrifices; and the glory of the LORD filled the house.*
> *And the priests could not enter into the house of the LORD, because the glory of the LORD had filled the house.*
> *And when all the children of Israel saw how the fire came down, and the glory of the LORD on the house, they bowed themselves with their faces to the ground upon the pavement, and worshipped, and praised the LORD, saying, For He is good; for His mercy endures forever.*

While we are talking about the Temple let's list the various items we have been shown which will take place after our Jesus returns to reign and the millennium begins. This listing will help us get at-ease with the concept of that new day which is coming.

* All men, not with the seal of God in their foreheads, will be painfully tormented to the point of wanting death for up to five months. This takes place with probably forty days left in the Great Tribulation.

So this pain will last *three and half more months into the millennium*. Since it will, it will be the principal motivator to get the nations to all travel to Jerusalem to ask King Jesus for their healing. While there ... they will be 'separated' into the sheep and goat nations.

* The fowl-cleaned bones of the kings of the earth will, along with their vast armies, be found, gathered, and buried by Jesus' servants until the seventh month of the first year.

* Jesus will oversee the construction of the 'Third Temple' and of its priestly cleansing for service. Its prophesied opening date will be slightly more than six years and three months into the millennium..

* For seven years the huge amounts of weapons from the armies of the last battle will be found and burned for heat.

In other words, everyday life will proceed as naturally as it does for us today. The wonderful exception being that our Lord Jesus will be the world's King, ruling in Jerusalem and ruling in righteousness! And Satan will also be bound. So, he will not be able to mastermind his evil plots against the nations of the earth as he has been able to do in our lifetimes.

The earth will be more or less at peace with itself.

Its animal population will once again experience a more sane and peaceful relationship among themselves. All the creation of living beings will experience the extremely long and productive lives they did before the Flood.

The Beginning

The 'end of the present age' in which we are living, and the at-the-same-moment-coming of our Lord Jesus, will usher in the beginning of the new age: the Millennium. They will usher in the one thousand year long Lord's Day.

The Lord's Day actually begins on the day that the wicked abomination of desolation is placed in the holy place. It is then that our Lord God Almighty begins acting as if He was the only One in control. *He has relinquished that right for far too long.* But on that Day no one elses' dictates matter.

Only His desires count from that day forth.

As He said to the fowls of the air through Ezekiel:

> *Come, gather yourselves on every side to My*
> *sacrifice that I do sacrifice for you, even a*
> *great sacrifice upon the mountains of Israel.*
> *You shall eat...till you be full, and drink*
> *...till you be drunken of My sacrifice which*
> *I have sacrificed for you.*
> *Thus shall you be filled at My table with*
> *horses and chariots, with mighty men and with*
> *all men of war, saith the Lord GOD.*

John instructs us it is the *great supper of God*...the fowls and beasts of Ezekiel's vision were informed it is the *great sacrifice of God*. In both instances it is God, *and God alone*, Who is in charge.

The puny kings of this world and the Antichrist are not in any control at all. Oh, they will be going about as if they are in complete control. But He 'Who sits in the Heavens' shall laugh at them. For what they really are are puny, puny, puny ants and fleas in His sight.

Those of you who have heard author Frank Peretti do his unique impersonation of one famous actress': *"I am god! I am god!"* in the punyiest, tinniest voice imaginable can get a good prespective of what is happening in the Middle East especially at time of the second coming of our Lord Jesus.

The beast of Revelation (ie, the Antichrist) and all of his co-horts will act so big and mighty, and will in actuality be just an puny little irritant to our Lord God Almighty.

Just a puny little irritant.

If you know the Almighty One, the everlasting Creating God

of the heavens and the earth, then never, never, never, fear the Lord's Day.

Pray for the Lord's Day.

Plead with our Lord God Himself to begin taking back the control of this old planet for HIS glory and for HIS own good pleasure.

Pray for that daily.

When He does....

Satan Bound

Satan will be bound.

All who follow Satan and his way will be destroyed.

Isn't that a day to which we all look forward?

I say that, and I TRULY believe that, Satan does not even know that I exist. Since he is not omniscient like our Lord, I believe his interests have to be focused toward Israel ... and the large metropolitan centers of this world where he likes to think he rules. But even a lowly, non-known one like me...oh, I long for the day that that evil one will no longer be able to continue to mess up the countries of our world with his lying, deceptive ways.

Therefore, praise God!

Satan will be 'laid hold upon' by our Lord Jesus Christ and that devil will be bound and cast into the bottomless pit for an entire Lord's Day. Oh, Glory! What a relief that will be for this old world.

For a full DAY!

For 1000 years!

And to think that Satan "began as the anointed cherub that covers, and that he was upon the holy mountain of God,...and that he was perfect in all his ways from the day that he was created UNTIL INIQUITY WAS FOUND IN HIM." See Ezekiel 28:14-15.

What a sad commentary.

What a waste of a wonderful being.

Pride, envy, greed...did him in.

Our Lord Jesus will bound that serpent and rid this world of him for ONE FULL DAY in our God's reckoning.

For one thousand years.

Jesus casts him into the 'bottomless pit' and shuts him up, and sets a seal upon him that he should deceive the nations no more, until the thousand years should be fulfilled: after that he must be loosed a little season.

Satan Loosed! Why?

When the thousand years are expired, Satan shall go out to deceive the nations which are in the four quarters of the earth, 'Gog and Magog,' to gather them together to battle: the number of whom is as the sand of the sea.

Do you get what I, John, am saying?

The devil HAS to be loosed AFTER our Lord Jesus reigns 1000 years: because during those 1000 years there are so many who have not gloried in living under King Jesus' leadership and under His righteousness.

It will be even as in the kingdom of heaven that Jesus set up in the beginning of our age ... that 'final kingdom' is going to be loaded with TARES. It will be filled with 'millions' of men and women who never-ever really wanted to leave behind their own wants and their own leadership in their lives.

Satan will thus be freed to deceive all those who truly are of the 'ilk' to go their own way. Finally, all those deceived men and women will be gathered from all over the world against the righteous in the beloved city. Again God Himself will step in.

He will destroy them. He will send fire down on them just like He destroyed the Assyrians who surrounded that same city back in the days of Hezekiah!

Bye, Bye, Satan

The destroying fire of course did not devour Satan.

Instead, he will be cast into the same lake of fire which the Antichrist and false prophet were flung into at the beginning of the reigning of Jesus.

They shall be tormented day and night forever and ever and ever.

The Final Judgment

After that I saw a great white throne.

A great white judgment throne.

The initial 'judgment' was the sending away of the corrupt earth and its heavens. Corrupted because of Satan's conceit and his causing mankind to rebel against the rule and 'life' of God. Corrupted because such vast and monumental judgments had to be poured out upon it so many times. Corrupted by the very ones who were to be so blessed by its existence.

This rebellious sphere was not to have any part in God's new beginnings.

Next, I saw the dead, small and great (READ: ALL), stand before God.

The books were opened.

Another book was opened.

It was a solemn moment.

That last book was the book of life...*the book of life!* I was so intrigued by its very concept.

All those dead, both the small and great, were judged out of those things which were written in the first books I saw. They were judge according to their works.

There was not any place where all the dead were which did not give up its dead for this time of judgment. And ALL were, as I wrote above, judged according to their works.

However, having one's NAME written in that final book I mentioned was the only criteria for knowing at 'where' each and everyone would be spending the rest of eternity.

---

*Whosoever was not found written in the
book of life was cast into the lake of fire.*

Where they lived in eternity was BASED on only that one criteria: whether one's name was in the book of life or not. Once that was determined all were still judged according to their works to determine the 'weighing' in which *few and many stripes* will be the judgment; and, for which, it will be **'more tolerable'** for some than it will for others in that day of judgment.

The Main Criteria:

IS YOUR

NAME

WRITTEN

IN THE BOOK

OF LIFE

10 + FIVE

New Heaven And New Earth

Then I saw a new heaven and a new earth!

I saw no more sea on the new earth.

I saw the holy city, *'New Jerusalem'*, come down from God out of Heaven. It was beautifully prepared as a bride adorned for her husband.

And I heard a great voice from Heaven saying, Behold, **the 'tabernacle of God' is with men.** He shall dwell with them. They shall be His people, and He Himself shall be with them. He shall be their God.

He shall wipe away all tears from their eyes.

There shall be no more death.

Nor sorrow.

Nor crying.

Neither shall there be any more pain.

For the former things of this world are passed away.

God upon His throne says: Behold, I make all things new.

He told me to write:

these words are true and faithful.

He also added:

**It is done. I am
Alpha and Omega,
the beginning and the end.
I will give unto him that is athirst
of the fountain of the water of life freely.
He that overcomes shall inherit all things
and I will be his God and he shall be My son.**

**But the fearful and unbelieving and the abominable,
and murderers, and whoremongers, and sorcerers,
and idolaters, and all liars, shall have
their part in the lake which burns
with fire and brimstone.**

Next, one of those seven angels which had the seven vials came unto me on a mission. He spake, "Come here, I will show you the Bride: the Lamb's wife." And he carried me away in the spirit to a great and high mountain, and showed me that great city, the holy Jerusalem, descending out of Heaven from God.

What can I say, friends?

It had the glory of God.

Its light was like unto a stone most precious, even like a jasper stone, clear as crystal.

It had a wall, great and high.

It had twelve gates...and at the gates twelve angels.

On the gates NAMES were written which are the names of the twelve tribes of the children of Israel.

There were three gates on each of the four sides of the great wall...three on the east, three on the north, three on the south, and three on the west.

The great wall of the city had twelve foundations.

I began to weep.

My name was there!

In the twelve foundations of the city were the names of the twelve apostles of the Lamb. Oh, thank you, Lord.

The Angel Measured The City With A Golden Reed

The new city lay foursquare. Each side was twelve thousand furlongs...as was its height! The great wall around the city was one hundred and forty-four cubits. It was built of jasper.

The city was built of pure gold, like unto clear glass.

The foundations were adorned with precious stones:

(1) jasper, (2) sapphire, (3) chalcedony, (4) emerald (5) sardonyx, (6)sardius, (7) chrysolyte, (8)beryl, (9)topaz (10) chrysoprasus, (11) jacinth, and (12) amethyst.

The twelve gates of the great wall were pearls. Each gate was one pearl!

The streets of the city were pure gold! They were as if they were transparent glass!

No Temple In The City

I saw no Temple in the city for the Lord God Almighty and the Lamb are the Temple in it. The city had no need of the sun or the moon to shine in it. The glory of the Lord lightens the city. The Lamb also is the light of it.

The nations which are saved, and are therefore on the earth, shall walk in the light of the city. They will no longer need the sun or moon for their light.

The kings of the earth—all righteous of course—will bring their glory and honor into the city. Its twelve gates, those large pearl gates, will not be shut at all by day ... and there never shall be be any night there. Thus the kings will continuously bring the glory and honor of the nations into the city.

Without a doubt, there will never, never, be anything which can defile or work abomination or make a lie that shall ever be allowed to enter the city. The Presence of the Lord makes it an impossible-possibility.

Only those who are written in the Lamb's book of life: only they can enter into the city of God.

That is amazing. What else could that fact mean except that even in the new heaven and new earth THERE is again going to be the possibility of a *'fall'* of some kind. And, that if there is, none of those 'fallen' beings will ever be allowed into the new Jerusalem. It will be even as we in our age have no chance now of entering into Heaven.

When our Father creates, He never, *but never*, eliminates the possibility of allowing His longsuffering and mercy to be brought into play. (I believe He is constantly creating out at the very 'ultimate' limits of His ability. Please do not fault me for having that thought of our Father.)

The River Of Life

The angel showed me a pure river flowing with the water of life. That river of course was as clear as crystal. It proceeded out of the throne of God and of the Lamb itself.

Also in that city, on either side of the river, was the TREE OF LIFE!

The tree of life was in the city!

Why did Adam not choose that tree, I will never know. The tree bares twelve kinds of fruits. It yields those fruit in EVERY month. Its leaves were for the healing of the nations.

I simply loved the city, the New Jerusalem, and everything I saw and heard about it.

With the eradication of the old heavens and earth there also went the old curse. May I repeat: there shall be no more curse. How wonderful that sounds! In the new heavens and new earth and in the city there shall be no more of Adam's curse!

The throne of God and of the Lamb shall be there.

All His servants shall serve Him.

They shall see His face.

His name shall be in the forehead of each of them.

They shall reign with Him for ever and ever.

Of course they will not even need candles there.

The angel wanted to be certain that I realized that all I was seeing was for real. "These sayings I have been giving you are faithful and true," he told me adding, "the Lord God of the holy prophets sent his angel to show unto his servant and servants the things which must shortly come to pass."

BEHOLD

BEHOLD I COME QUICKLY

QUICKLY

Blessed is he that keeps the sayings of the prophecy of this book. I, John, saw these things and heard them.

When I did, I fell down to 'worship' before the feet of the angel which showed me these things.

"NO! See that you do not do it!" he cried at me. "For I am your fellow servant, and of your brethren the prophets, and of them which keep the sayings of this book. Worship God."

I pondered that: he was my fellow servant.

Who was this one.

He was 'of' my brethren the prophets.

I was being shown around Heaven by a former brother, by a former prophet.

By one who had, like us, kept the sayings of the book.

Then, unlike Daniel near the end of his book, the angel said to me, "Seal NOT the sayings of the prophecy of this book: for the time is at hand. He that is unjust, let him be unjust still; he that is filthy, let him be filthy still; he that is righteous, let him be righteous still; and he that is holy, let him be holy still."

It sounded so much like the words to Daniel: many shall be purified & made white & tried; but the wicked shall do wickedly: and none of the wicked shall **'understand'**, but the wise shall understand." This Messenger had to be Jesus. He had to be the same One Who told Daniel those identical words. Of course He was before me as a messenger, but it had to be Him. It had to be. And...and...at that moment He said:

**AND, BEHOLD, I COME QUICKLY;
AND MY REWARD IS WITH ME,
TO GIVE TO EVERY MAN ACCORDING
AS HIS WORK SHALL BE.**

**I AM ALPHA AND OMEGA,
THE BEGINNING AND THE END,
THE FIRST AND THE LAST.**

Blessed are they that do God's commandments that they may have right to the tree of life, and may enter in through the gates into the city. For outside the gates are dogs, and sorcerers and whoremongers and murderers and idolaters and whosoever loves and makes a lie. (Like I realized earlier, always, always, in His creations is the possibility of those coming into it who will not obey or will not put their trust in Him. In this case, as in the first creation, these evil, selfish ones will not be allowed to gain access to God Himself or to the tree of life.

The Messenger spoke again:)

I

JESUS

HAVE SENT MINE ANGEL
TO
TESTIFY UNTO YOU
THESE THINGS IN THE CHURCHES.

I AM

THE ROOT AND THE OFFSPRING OF DAVID, AND THE BRIGHT AND MORNING STAR.

This again is a to-the-churches statement. Jesus definitely did not testify these things to the people of Israel. All the words of His angel which I have shared throughout this scroll were to be testified *in the churches*. This largest prophetic book which will be included in all the writings of the apostles and leaders in the churches of Jesus Christ is *for the churches*. It is not for Israel. It is for the churches, brethren.

That is the word of Jesus.

The Spirit And The Bride Say,

"Come"

And let him that hear say, **"Come."**

YES

COME

LORD JESUS!

And, let him that is athirst ***come***...and whosoever will, let him take the water of life freely. For I testify to every man that hears the words of the prophecy of this book:

> *If any man shall add unto these things*
> *God shall add unto him the plagues that*
> *are written in this book.*
> *If any shall take away from the words of*
> *the book of this prophecy, God will take away*
> *his part out of the holy city and from the*
> *things that are written in this book.*

He which testifies these things says:

SURELY

I COME

QUICKLY

Amen!
Even so, come, Lord Jesus.
The grace of our Lord Jesus Christ be with you all.

AMEN!

10 + SIX

♥ ♥ ♥ ♥ ♥ ♥ ♥ ♥ ♥ ♥
♥ ♥ ♥ ♥ ♥ ♥ ♥ ♥ ♥
♥ ♥ ♥ ♥ ♥ ♥

Old Milkman And His Horse

To close this first book on God's Game Plan, I will use an illustration that I recently heard a preacher give in one large independent church in Indiana. His purpose of offering this tale was for a different reason than I will ... he used it to show how we have to allow our new Master to lead us in much different paths, in paths of righteousness, once we become born again and we no longer have our old man as the master of our lives.

My reason, though different, will be quite as apparent.

There was an old milkman who had, back in the days of the horse-drawn vehicles, one horse which had 'faithfully served' him for his entire life as a route delivery man. The horse was so used to the same route year after year that often the milkman would fall asleep once the last delivery had been made...and the horse would obediently carry him back home.

One day the milkman died.

The horse and cart were sold. A doctor bought them because he was quite impressed how faithfully this horse had served the milkman. The doctor found to his dismay, however, that every time he hooked the old horse and buggy up to make his rounds of his patients that the horse always wanted to go the 'old' milk route which it knew so well.

The horse, which had never had a need to feel the reins and the whip with the milkman, then began to feel those instruments as the doctor had to train him over to do his own bidding.

We are like that horse. We have learned some 'trib' position dealing with the Prophetic Puzzle, and if that position begins to falter and have holes in it, you and I will often have to 'feel the reins and whip' before we will follow the new Master's lead.

On the other hand, those who are willing to proceed with the leading of a new master, the prophetic scriptures will give you years and decades of new enjoyment to pursue.

To you I offer these new 'wine skin' charts:

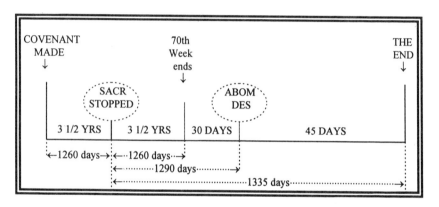

Above is Daniel's 70th week with the added days.
Below is the same with the Great Tribulation shown.

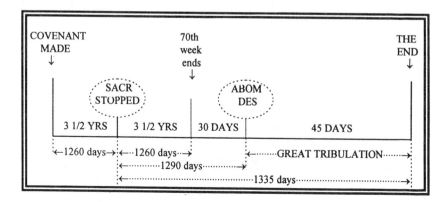

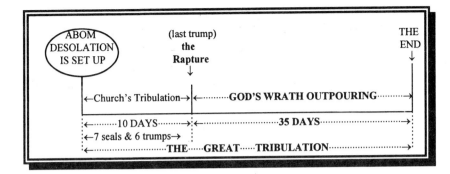

Above is the last 45 days (*The Great Tribulation*) with the seals and trumpets, and the Rapture, and the 35 days of Wrath (the vials) shown.

The Revelation would have miserably failed the progressive revelation test if it hadn't presented such a graphic, outstanding, complete picture of the church's being harvested Home by our Lord Jesus Christ.

The Revelation is not about Satan.

The Revelation is not about the Antichrist.

It says a little about them, but the primary & overwhelming thrust throughout the entire book is Jesus, Jesus, Jesus! This is God's Game Plan! And His Game Plan has always been to bring glory to His dearly beloved Son!

My Rapture Vision

Let me share with you a vision/dream I had.

It occurred in that 'almost-conscious-yet-still-asleep' part of near-awakeness. I seemed *'cognizant'* of what was happening, however, when I awoke I distinctly knew I wasn't awake when I saw the vision/dream.

It all happened very fast.

In the dream I was 'RUSHING BACKWARDS' at a high speed! First buildings, then skyscrapers were flinging past me as I WAS RUSHING upward away from this earth.

At that moment...at that instant...the thought came: *Do you want to continue coming to ME?*

Did I want to continue coming to Him? Of course!

And that SAME INSTANT a second thought immediately came: *You finally have a chance to possibly pastor a church. You have always had that as your DREAM to pastor a church.*

The choice was given me in an instant.

In a nanosecond.

And I awoke.

I mean, I came to on my bed.

FULLY AWAKE.

AND....

AND....

AND with my arms lifted straight for the ceiling!

Fully covered with goosebumps.

I cried with joy.

I cried with the clear, immediate understanding that in that moment before awakeness I had made the correct decsion.

I had said YES to Him.

I had accepted continuing going upward to Him—over the chance for WHAT I TRULY WANTED down here upon the earth.

I just lay there.

Thankful.

Ever so thankful.

The Thought Hit Me Hard

We may all have some similar choice INSTANTLY come into our minds at the very second of the rapture. A choice that will be: *you may come Home with Me...or hang onto the most cherished possession or dream you have here on this old earth.* The choice may be a very righteous one. But it's still a choice... going with Him may not be as automatic as we have thought it would be.

It was a vision/dream. It was not scripture. So of course it is debatable. However, from that day to this one, I have never felt that participating in the Rapture would be as automatic as I had thought it would be before having experienced that dream.

Friends, it may not be, but it may be, that WE will all have that *'nanoinstant'* to choose if we want to go with Him or not. And the choice could seem to be an exceedingly righteous one. But be not deceived, our saying 'YES' to staying here for any reason will be a definite 'NO' to Him for going to be with Him as He gathers and takes His Bride back to His Father..

If we stay we of course will go into the wrath portion of the great tribulation which immediately follows the offer of being in the Rapture...and we will be martyred for our faith. And that may be the reason we were to stay here. (God does not seem to judge them that remain here and are martyred for their faith.)

But if we choose at that nanoinstant to go with Him. We go AS HIS BRIDE. *Obviously we know Jesus' will in this matter:*

I GO TO PREPARE A PLACE FOR YOU.
AND IF I GO AND PREPARE A PLACE FOR YOU,
I WILL COME AGAIN AND RECEIVE YOU UNTO
MYSELF;
THAT WHERE I AM, THERE YOU MAY BE ALSO
And
FATHER, I WILL THAT THEY ALSO,
WHOM YOU HAVE GIVEN ME, BE WITH ME
WHERE I AM; THAT THEY MAY BEHOLD MY
GLORY,
WHICH YOU HAVE GIVEN ME: FOR YOU LOVED
ME BEFORE THE FOUNDATION OF THE
****WORLD****

After all that He has done for us, how can we do less than raise our hands and gladly seek to rise to Him when He calls our name.

How can we do less?

Should I begin numbering the reasons?

The new house we finally were able to get.

The new "We wanted it all our life" car we finally have in our drive.

Our wedding is next week!

Our baby is almost here.

When Jesus named the excuses people were giving Him for not following Him in His day, they were just as common. But they hurt Him just as much. Knowing all that He has to give all who will follow Him, it truly grieves Him when we will accept ANY reason for not going to be with Him as His followers and disciples and Bride.

I've Had Two Other Vision/Dreams.

They were completely identical. But they happened months apart. I saw a brilliant *'dot'* in the center of my mind's viewing, and that *light-spot* would speed toward me and instantly fill the entire screen of my mind.

Again the first thought: THIS IS JESUS COMING!

The second thought: *But you finally are on the verge of....*

Both those times I woke up with my arms raised straight up toward the ceiling, covered with big goosebumps.

I was ever so grateful for my response, but each time I was devastated that I wasn't actually on my way UPWARD.

Both times the scenes had been so real I was certain I was on my way UP (even as I was in the former dream I mentioned first). Both times I stayed in bed for a mighty long time. Stayed there to think for awhile. Stayed there to reflect on what each particular vision meant at that time in my life.

Those are the only three visions I have had dealing with the Rapture. All dealt with the actual instant of the reaping by Jesus. All relayed the message that there would be a choice we would have to make instantly and correctly, if we truly wanted to be included in that greatest of all days yet in our future.

There is no way I can state for certain that is indeed GOING TO BE THE CASE. Maybe it will be 'automatic' as most of us have believed it will be.

And maybe it won't.

Maybe we will have to choose at that instant.

No matter...let us just daily choose to follow Him, and then we will automatically choose rightly at that last trumpet's blow.

A Vision We Can All See

Let's all vividly see our Lord Jesus move slowly toward the throne in our own inner being. Let's watch Him walk up the stairs, turn around and seat Himself down upon the throne of our own life. Today, each day, let's pause to see that action by Him take place in our lives *each day.*

Then let's be the bride-to-be whose 'guy' is across the Seas. Our's of course has gone into a far country to receive for Himself a kingdom. And not just any oh kingdom...our Husband-to-be is there to receive an everlasting kingdom.

A kingdom in which He wants us to share the rule.

A kingdom in which righteousness is the ruling factor.

A kingdom in which no evil rulers can have a part.

Let's be the right kind of bride-to-be to Him.

Yes, He's far away (though He is ever so close!)

Yes, we can live anyway we want to.

Yes, the sky's the limit.

How foolish, friends, we would be to think that there is any other future Husband Who could ever be His equal. How foolish to even consider the idea of being unfaithful to Him.

But...many have.

Far too many have.

Hopefully the *hope* expressed by this book will help you to decide daily from this moment on to live exclusively for Him.

That is His desire.

He made it so clear far too many times for us to ever claim that we didn't really know that He wanted our undivided love and attention...that *He and His Father* so desire our undivided love and obedience.

Why else are They 'up there' preparing a magnificent Home for us...and that They have been at it for almost two thousand years already?

Why else...if it isn't because They SO LOVE US.

And THAT They do.

Their Word to us is so clear on it.

So very clear.

For God so loved the world that He gave His only-begotten Son that whosoever believes in Him should...have everlasting life.

Need we say anything else?

The Father loved us so much He GAVE us His wonderful Son as a sacrifice for our sins.

Jesus loved us so much He 'gave' us Himself that He might gain a spotless Bride for Himself.

The Spirit of God loves us so much that He has left Heaven for two thousand years so He can be 'here' to gather a pure and spotless Bride for the Son, for the very obedient Son.

And, friends, all the signs point to the truth that His sojourn here is almost over. All the signs point to the wonderful truth that He will soon be taking us back toward the Father's country so that we can 'meet' our Husband-to-be 'out in the field.'

And don't be concerned...the Son IS going to be out in the field intently watching for us. For no Man lays down His life for another...with no intention of 'one day' gathering that other one back to Himself.

It's all in God's Game Plan.

It's always been in His Game Plan.

Lord, we thank You for making known to us Your Game Plan in Your written Word.